Feathers, Fur and Flowers

Charles Ray

Uhuru Press
North Potomac, Maryland

The photographs in this book are the intellectual property of the author/photographer. Where identifiable persons are included in a photograph, appropriate approvals for publication have been obtained. If brands or logos appear in photos it is entirely inadvertent and does not imply endorsement by the author or publisher, nor does it imply that the brand or organization endorses this publication.

No part of this book may be copied or transmitted, by any means, without the express written consent of the copyright holder, except for fair use quotes in editorial reviews. For information on other works of the author, or to arrange speaking engagements, the author can be contacted at charlesray.author@gmail.com. The author's works can also be viewed on his web site, http://charlesray-author.com.

Independent authors survive based on the word-of-mouth buzz about their books, so if you like this work, please consider leaving a review, even a brief one, on the site where you bought it, on Amazon.com for instance, and on Goodreads.

Printed and manufactured in the United States of America by CreateSpace.

Copyright © 2018 Charles Ray

All rights reserved.

ISBN: 1987589688
ISBN-13: 978-1987589689

DEDICATION

This book is dedicated to the people who inspire me to create: my wife, Myung, who left Korea 42 years ago to begin a journey around the world with me, and is still on board; my two youngest (now in their forties) David and Denise, whose childish curiosity about the world around them inspired me to retain my own; and most importantly, the three currently most important people in my life, my grandchildren, Samantha Aeryn 'Sammie' Wickersham, Catherine Logan 'Catie' Wickersham, and Thomas Wesley 'Tommy' Wickersham, whose energy not only helps keep me going, but who have become my new favorite photographic subjects as I document their growing up..

CONTENTS

Acknowledgments	i
Introduction	1
Feathers	5
Fur	19
Flowers	43
Notes on Equipment, Techniques, Odds and Ends	53
Books by the author	57
About the author	61

ACKNOWLEDGMENTS

I grew up in a small farming town in East Texas where intellectual outlets were . . . well, lacking. For reasons that I've never understood, I've loved books, reading, art, and other intellectual trivia for as long as I can remember. By the time I was in fifth grade, for instance, I'd read every book in the school library—which, in retrospect, wasn't that much of a task, as they only had about a hundred books in total. My mother, Magnolia Gardner Alexander, and grandmother, Sally Young, though lacking in much formal education themselves, encouraged me to read, and spent their precious pennies buying me books and magazines. They both also encouraged my artistic wanderings, even when it involved pencil sketches on their good table cloths, or oil paint slopped on the carpet. Neither of them lived long enough to see the number of books I've published as an adult—my mother passed in 2002, just before I was confirmed to my first ambassadorial post, so she missed that as well—but, knowing them and their dogged East Texas persistence, they're somewhere looking down and smiling indulgently. Mom, grandma, this book's for you.

INTRODUCTION

I've been privileged to have been able to spend most of my adult life traveling and experiencing the world. I hadn't quite turned seventeen when I graduated from high school and left my small hometown in East Texas, with nothing more than my meager savings from working after school, a battered old suitcase containing my few clothes and a few of my favorite books, and a burning desire to see what the world was like beyond those pine-covered red hills.

Discovering that job opportunities in fields I'd like to work in, and was qualified for, were limited in the south in 1962 for a young black man and determined not to take work as a field hand or janitor, I joined the army as soon as I turned seventeen, which was the minimum age (with parental consent) for enlistment. I'd initially considered joining the Marine Corps, but the idea of spending so much time on ships was frightening, so I went to the army enlistment office instead. The funny thing about that is that just over six months later I found myself on an old Liberty-class cargo ship, leaving Brooklyn Harbor bound for Germany—and, of course, I got seasick the second day out of port, so it's a good thing I gave the marines a pass, I guess.

At any rate, over the next twenty years, until I retired from the army in 1982 as a seasoned major with two tours in Vietnam during the war, I saw a lot of the world. After leaving the army, I packed my wife and two young pre-school children, left Monterrey, California, and drove across country to join the U.S. Foreign Service and become a diplomat. For the next thirty years, I saw even more of the world, including places the army didn't normally send people, like Sierra Leone in West Africa or northeastern China, not far from the Arctic Circle.

In addition to a curiosity about the world, I've also been interested in artistic expression; painting, drawing, and photography. I think I might have inadvertently taken one of the first selfies when, as a four-year-old, I put my face in front of my mother's old Kodak Brownie and pressed the shutter release. Picture came out blurred and I got a spanking, but I think the click-click sound of that shutter releasing hooked me. I've been taking pictures, a lot of them really lousy, of places I've traveled since the beginning. I still have boxes of old black and white and color photographs, and color slides, which I keep promising myself I'll get converted to digital someday—maybe my grandchildren will do it after I'm gone. But, after I bought my first digital camera back in 2007, I've really documented my travels. My favorite subjects, other than snapping shots of interesting people and scenes from the window of my vehicle as I travel, is nature—plants, animals, landscapes.

In this book I have some of my favorite photographs of nature, the plants, animals, and scenes that have particularly impressed me. You will notice that the vast majority of them are from Africa, specifically southern Africa. I spent three years living in Zimbabwe, and I was absolutely floored by the amazing variety of wildlife, despite the fact that poaching and illegal hunting in endemic in the region. I've also included shots taken in other places. Northwestern Germany, for instance, the Mojave Desert in California, and, of course, around my home region, the northeastern United States, including Maryland, Virginia (both of which are technically considered part of the south, but I prefer to link them to the northeast), New York, and Pennsylvania.

Since 2007 I've taken thousands of digital pictures. I have thumb drives of them—and I've even lost a few drives—and, what you see here isn't even a drop in that bucket. It's more like a molecule of a drop.

I have more books like this planned over the coming months. But, that will depend upon readers like you giving me feedback. If you like this book, leave a review, even a brief 'atta boy' will do, on Amazon or Goodreads. That will tell me if it's worth the effort of combing through my drives and selecting and editing photos.

I do hope you'll enjoy these photos.

FEATHERS

Birds are among my favorite nature subjects, and the hardest to do. They hardly ever sit still, move erratically, and boy, are they fast. To me, though, that makes them all the more fascinating. I have a few photos here of birds in flight, but mostly, I've stalked them and snapped them when they decide to stay in one place for a while.

In these pages you'll find exotic birds of southern Africa, such as the grey heron, and common birds of North America, such as the robin and crow. The only difference that I've noticed between them, though, is where they're located. To a southern African, a cardinal would be as exotic and strange as some of the birds of that region are to us.

What you will notice here is that many of these photos were taken either in my backyard, or within a twenty-minute walk of my house. That's right, suburban Maryland has an astonishing variety of bird species, and many of them can be seen within the limits of major urban areas.

Some of the species pictured here I've been unable to identify. I include them anyway because I liked the photo, and perhaps some sharp-eyed reader will recognize them.

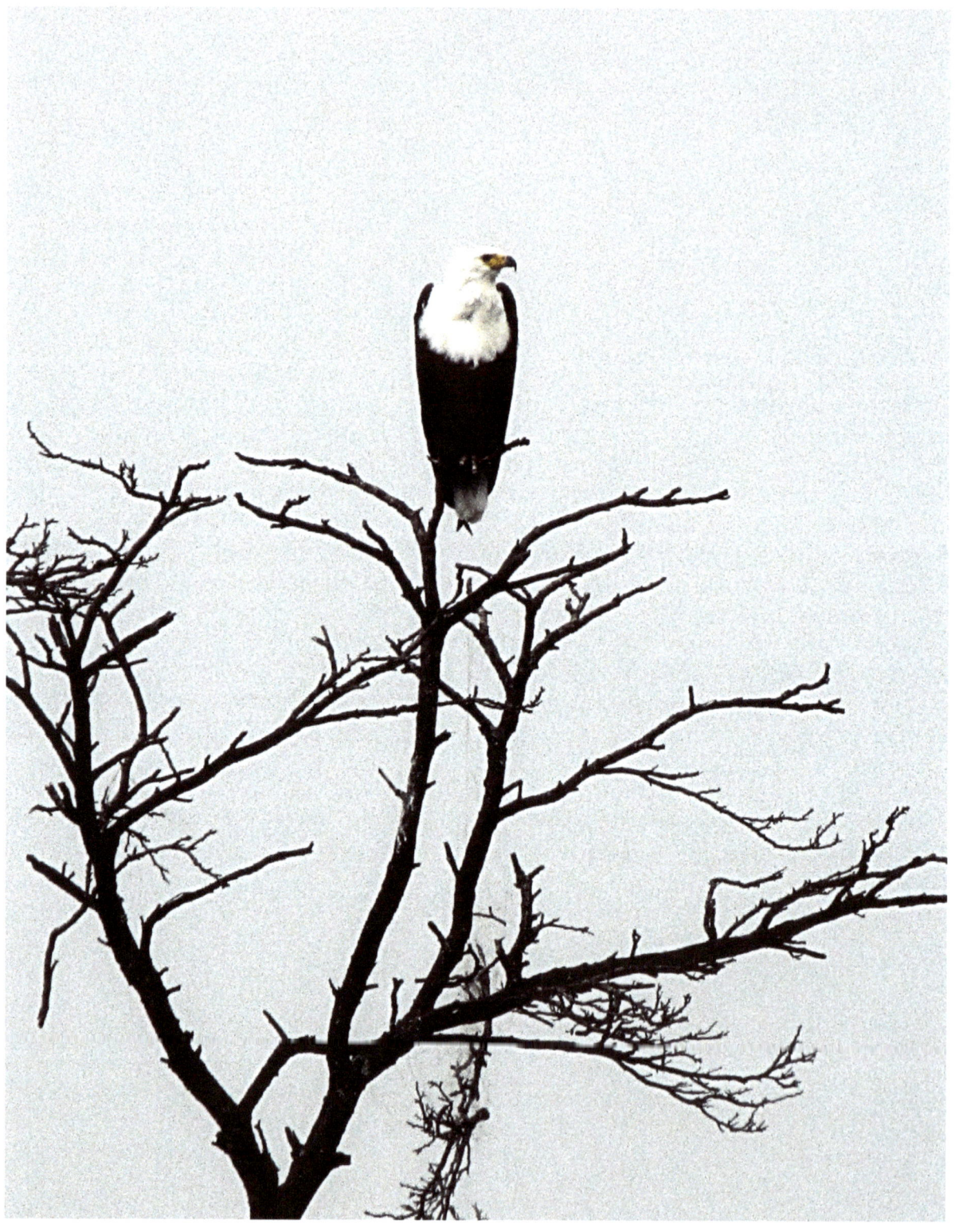

A fish hawk perched in the top of a tree next to a lake a few miles northwest of the Zimbabwean capital, Harare

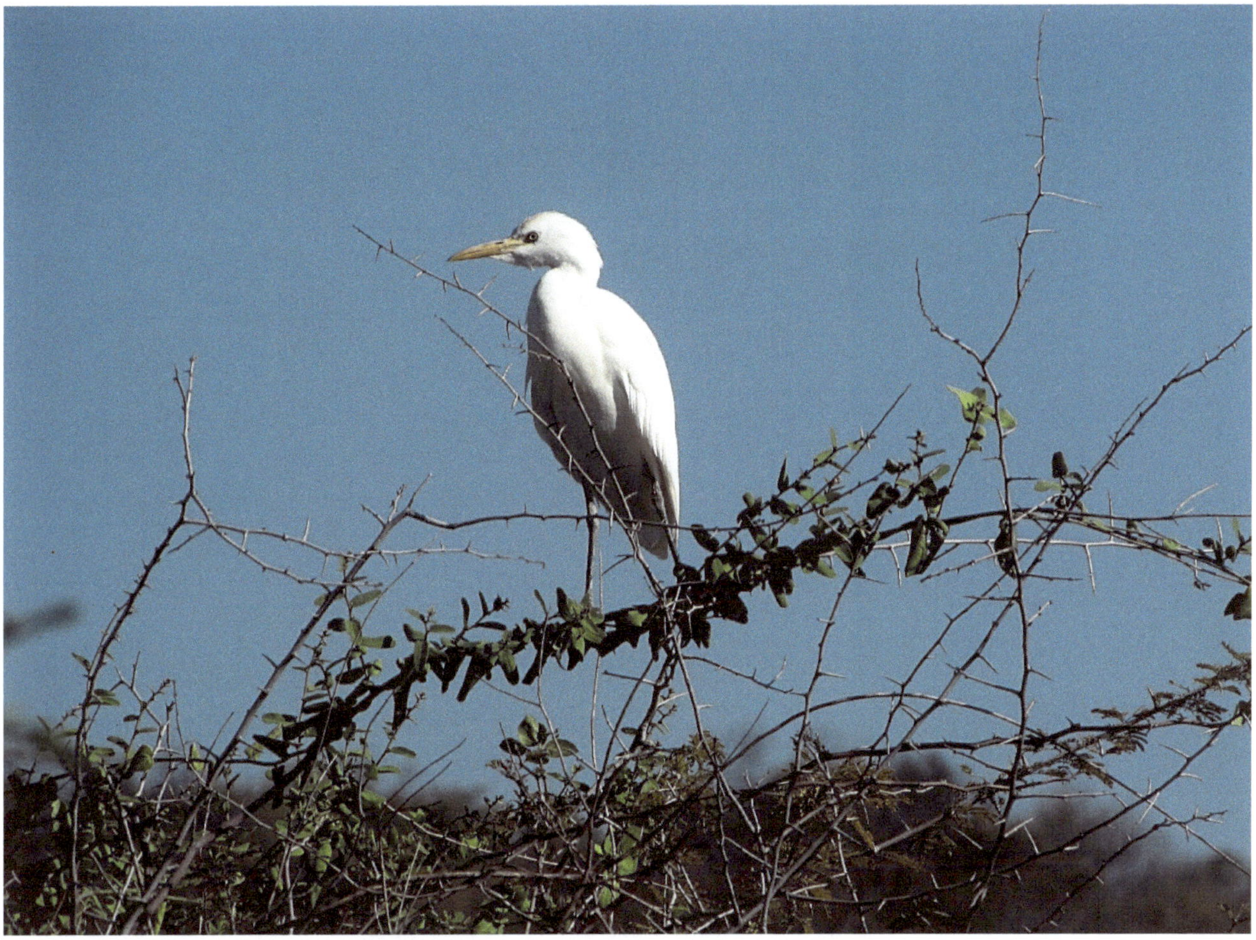

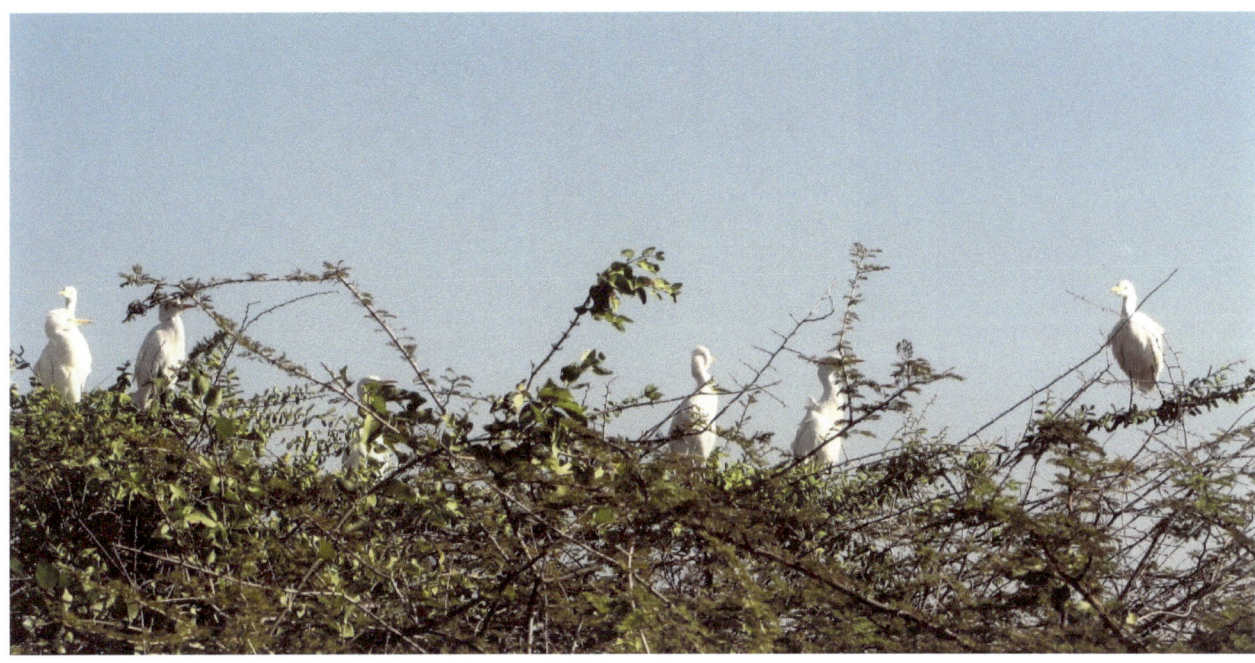

Great Egret in Zambezi Valley, Zimbabwe.

Flock of great egrets in Zambezi Valley, Zimbabwe

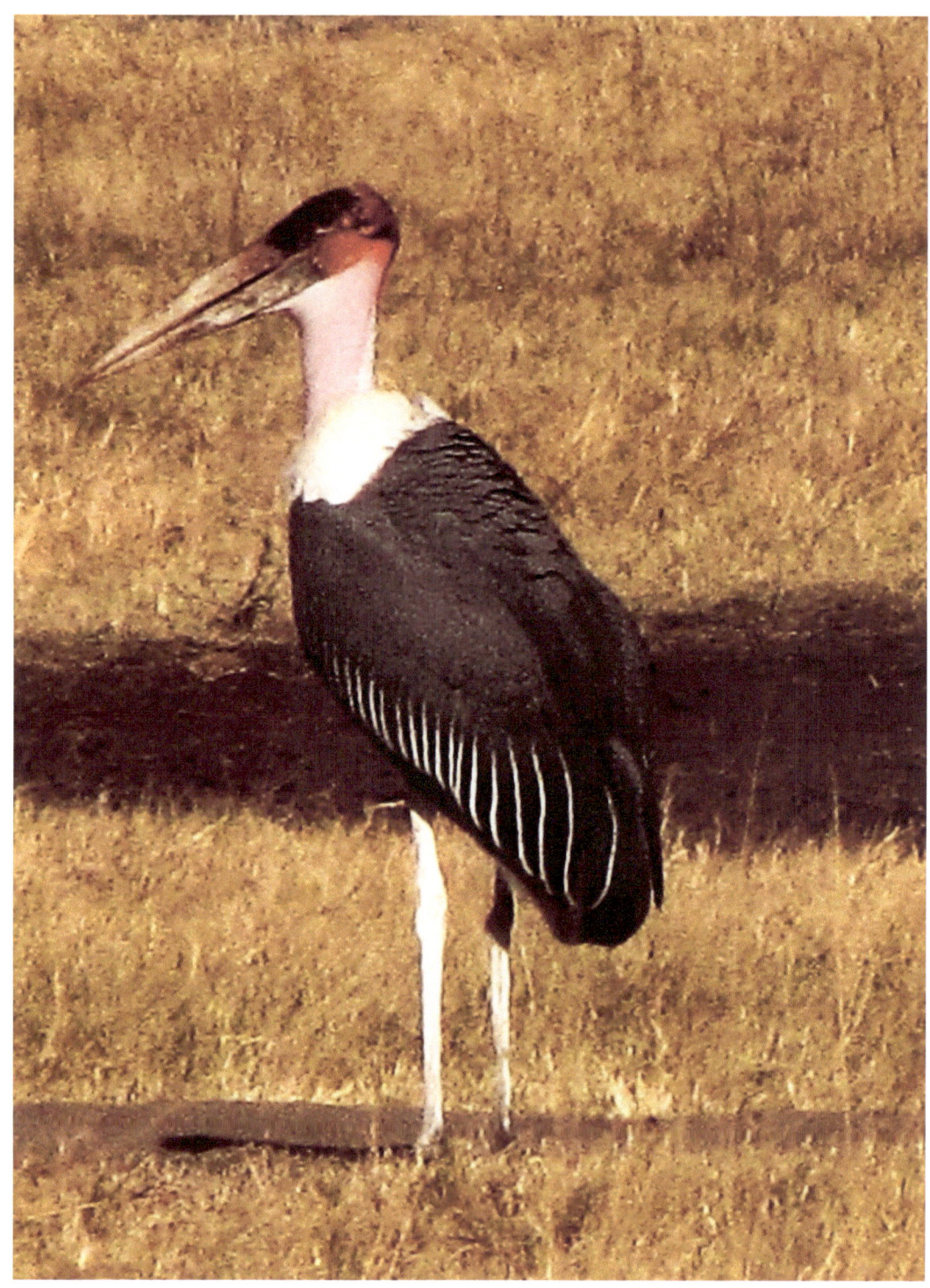

A marabou stork in Hwange, Zimbabwe.

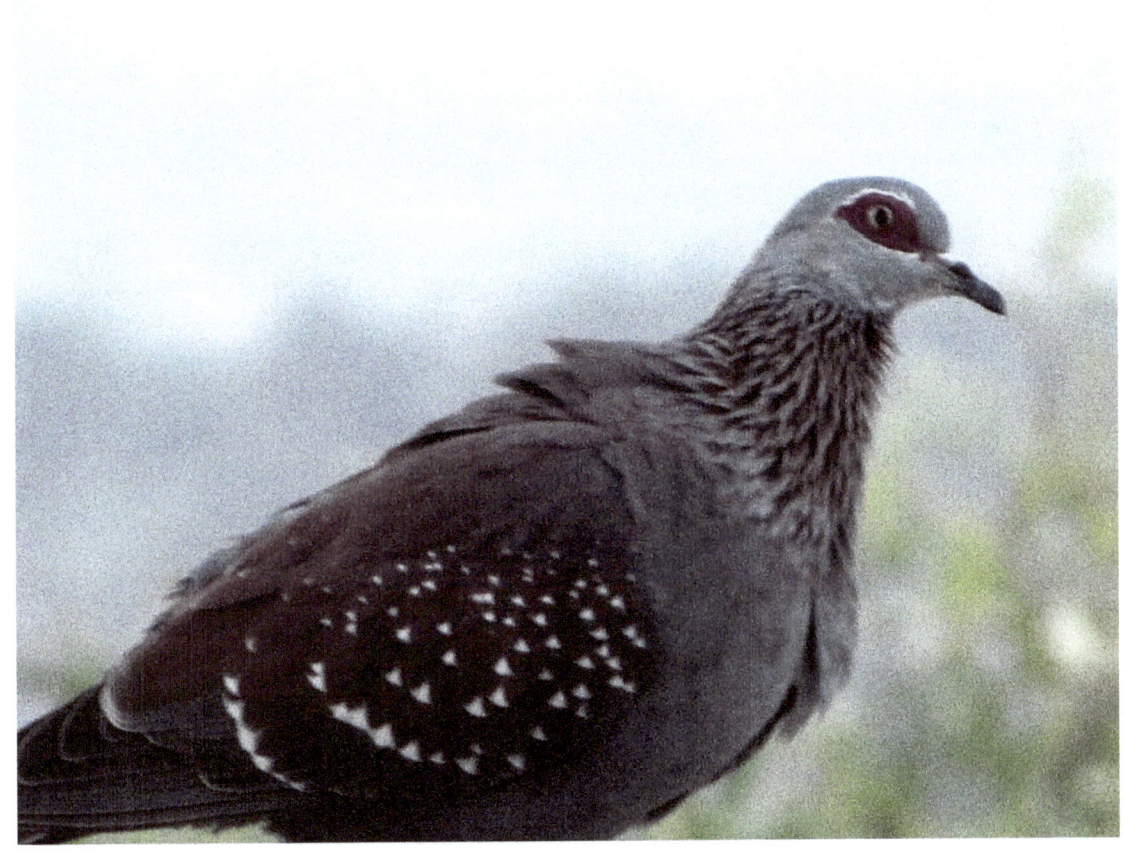

Speckled pigeon, Pretoria, South Africa

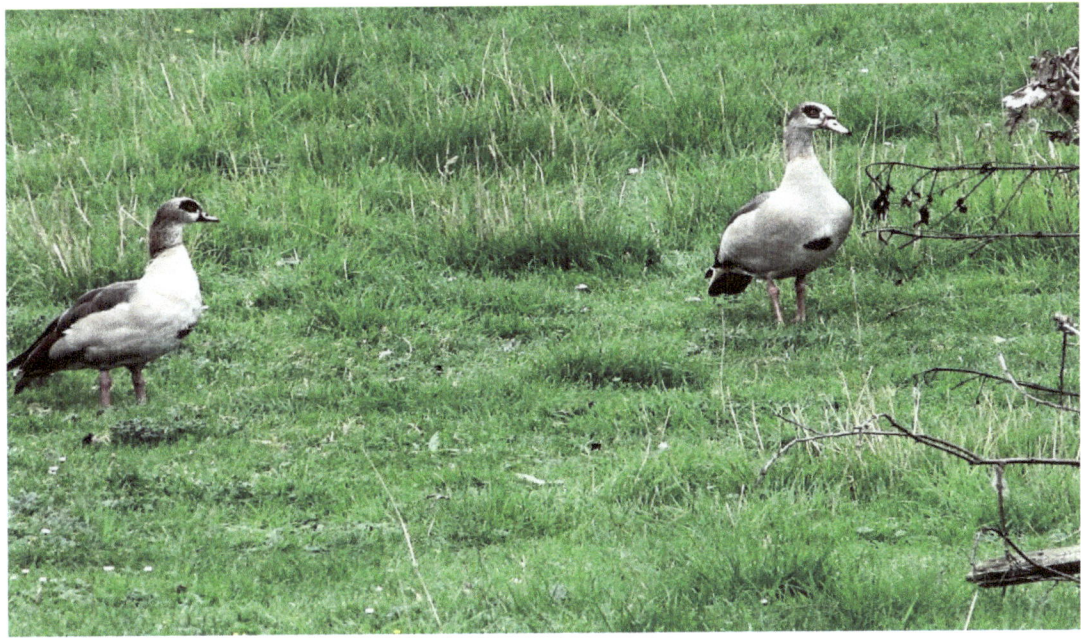

Moving farther north, two geese on a farm near Kleve, Germany.,

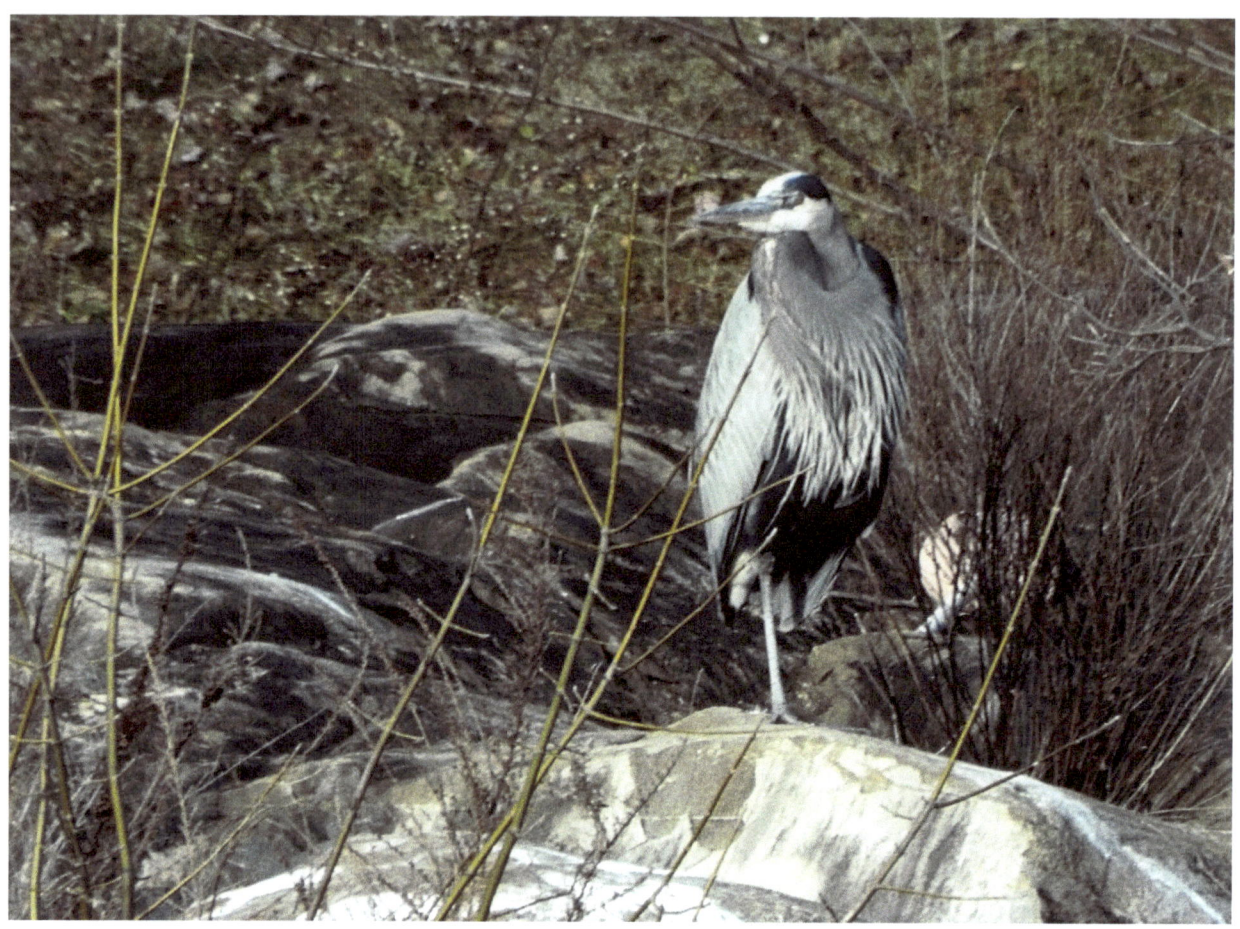

And, just show we have strange looking birds in the U.S., we cross the Atlantic for a look at this great blue heron nesting on a rock in a pond about two miles from my house in North Potomac, Maryland.

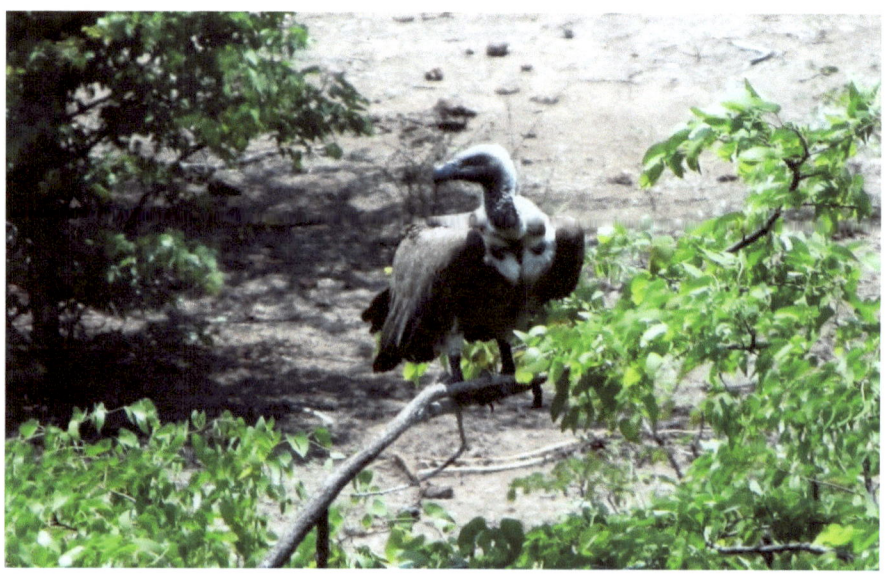

And then, back to Africa to see this vulture near a water hole at Victoria Falls, Zimbabwe.

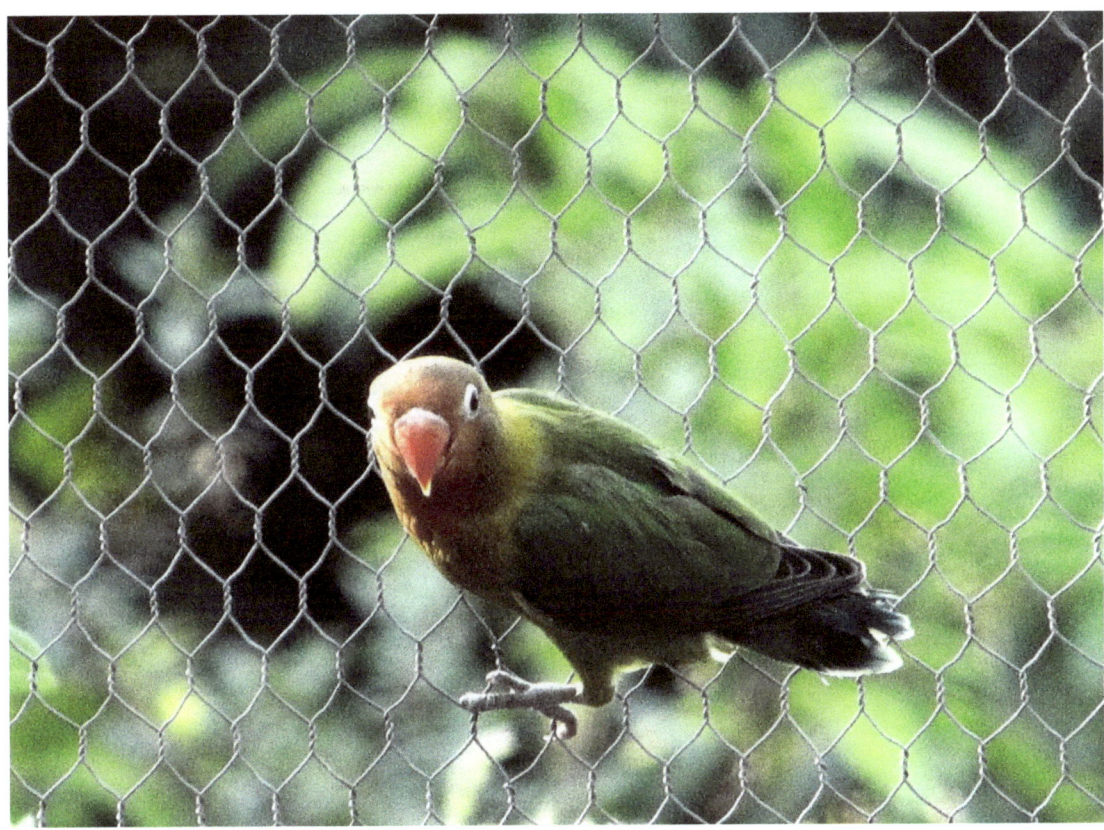

This Lilian's lovebird was in a game park in Hwange, Zimbabwe.

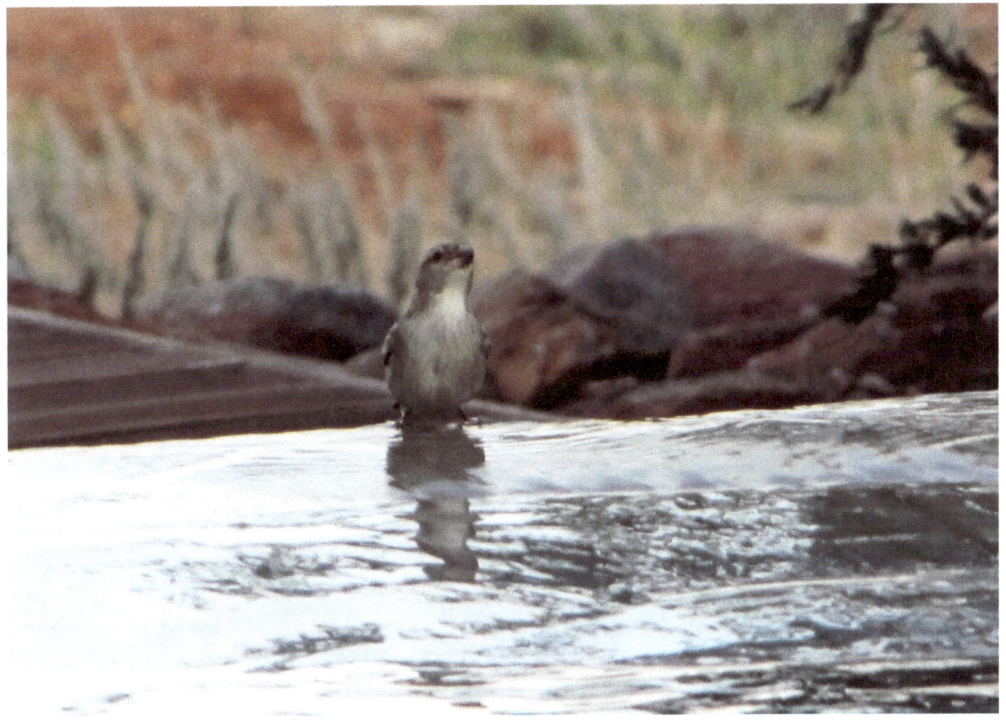

I was unable to identify the species of this little fellow who came to the patio-side fountain for a drink at the Tswalu Resort in South Africa's Kalahari Desert.

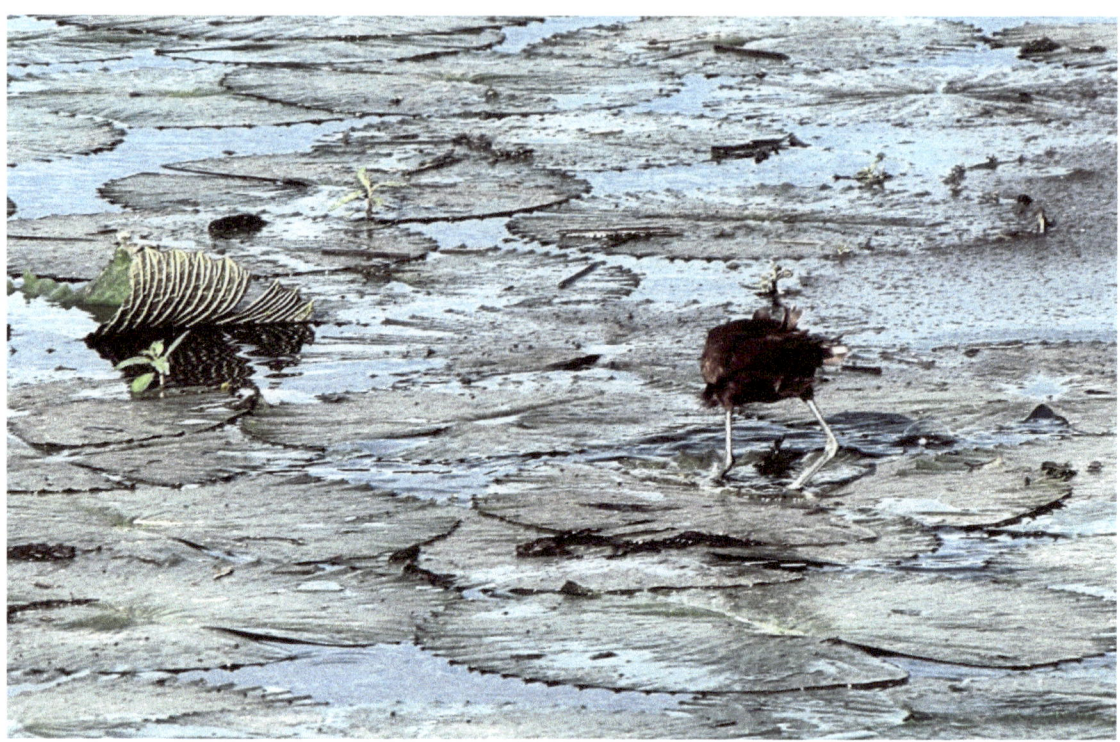

Another unidentified species on a lake in northeast Zimbabwe.

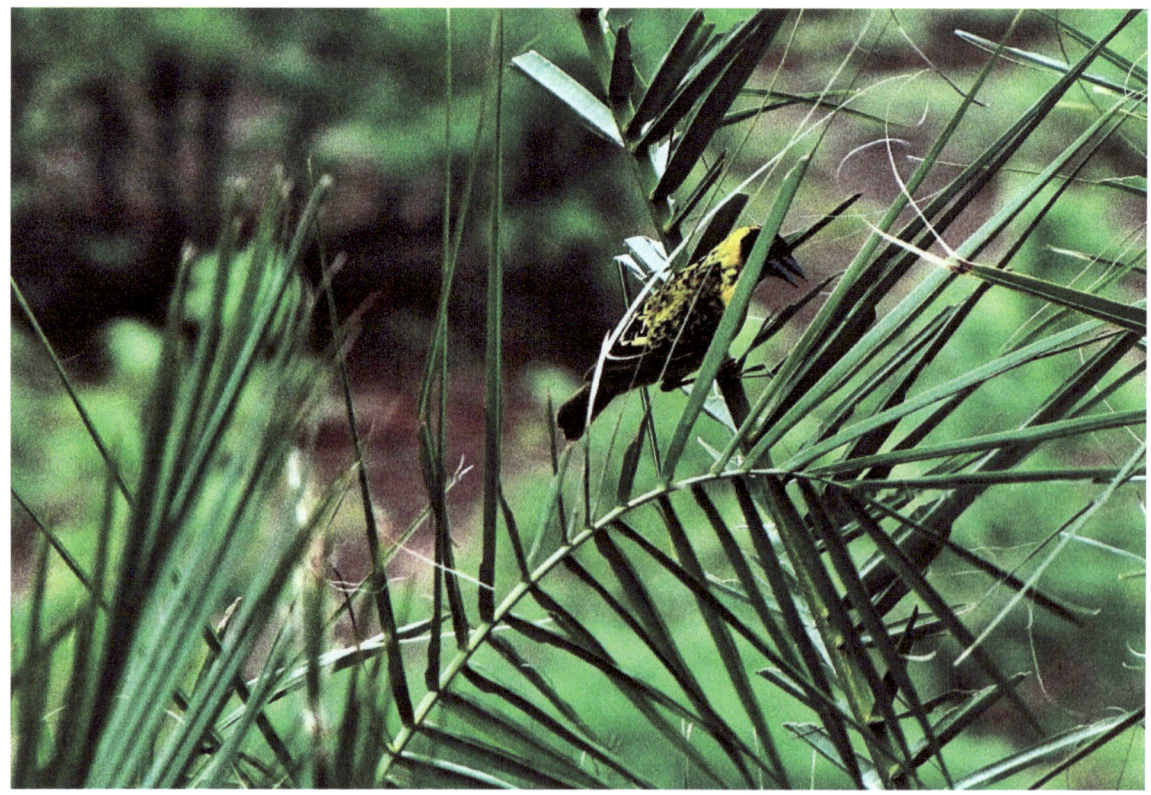

An interesting yellow bird, seen near Tswalu. Again, species unidentified.

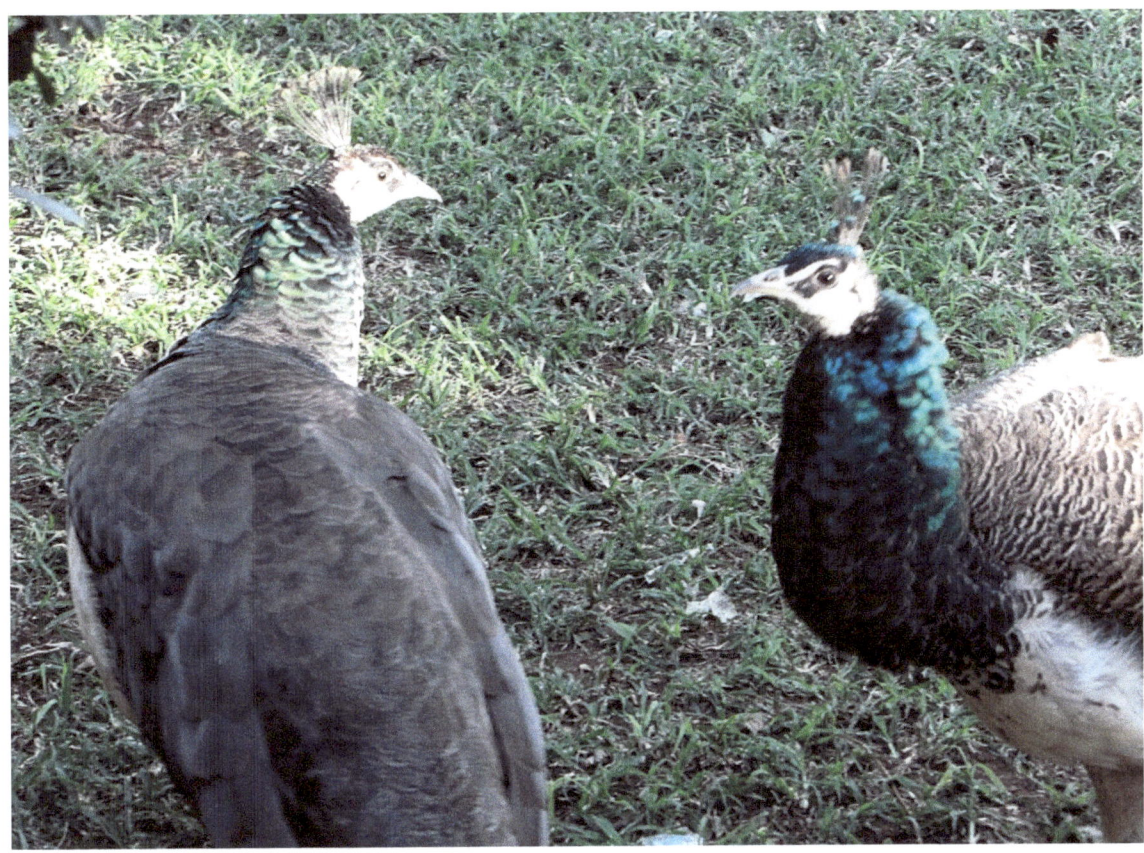

These two look a lot like crested peafowl. Seen at Bulawayo, Zimbabwe.

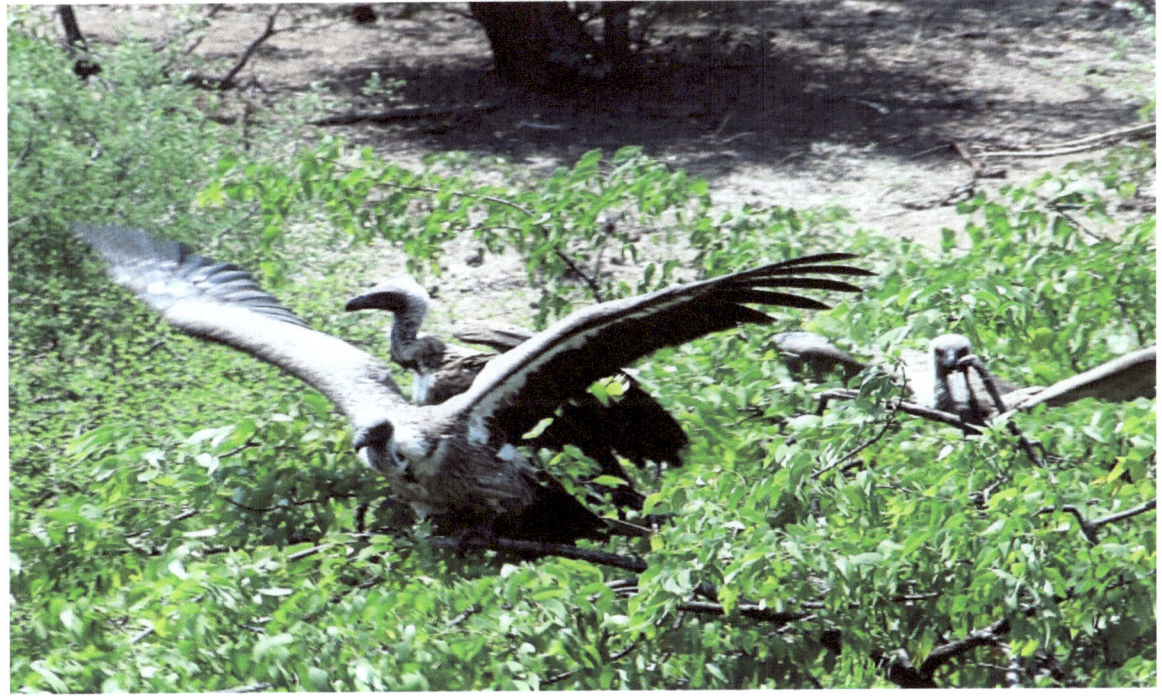

And, back to my favorites, the vultures. Ugly, but at the same time, graceful.

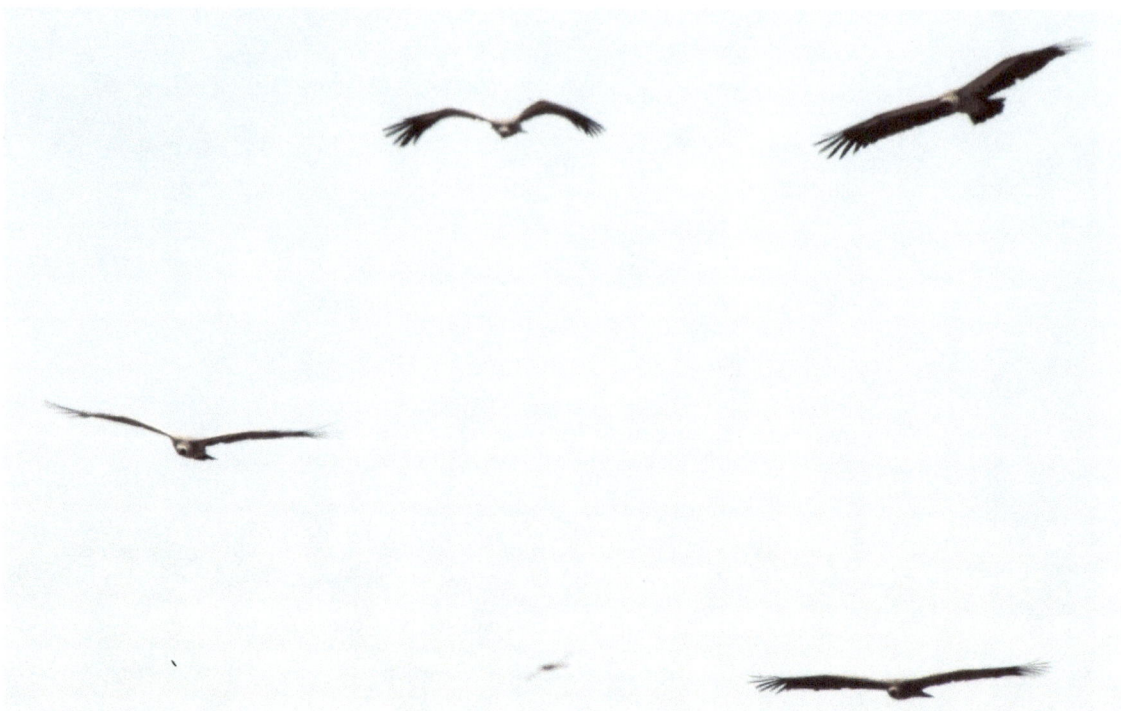

This is what I mean about the beauty of vultures in flight. It's only when they're on the ground that they look ugly to me.

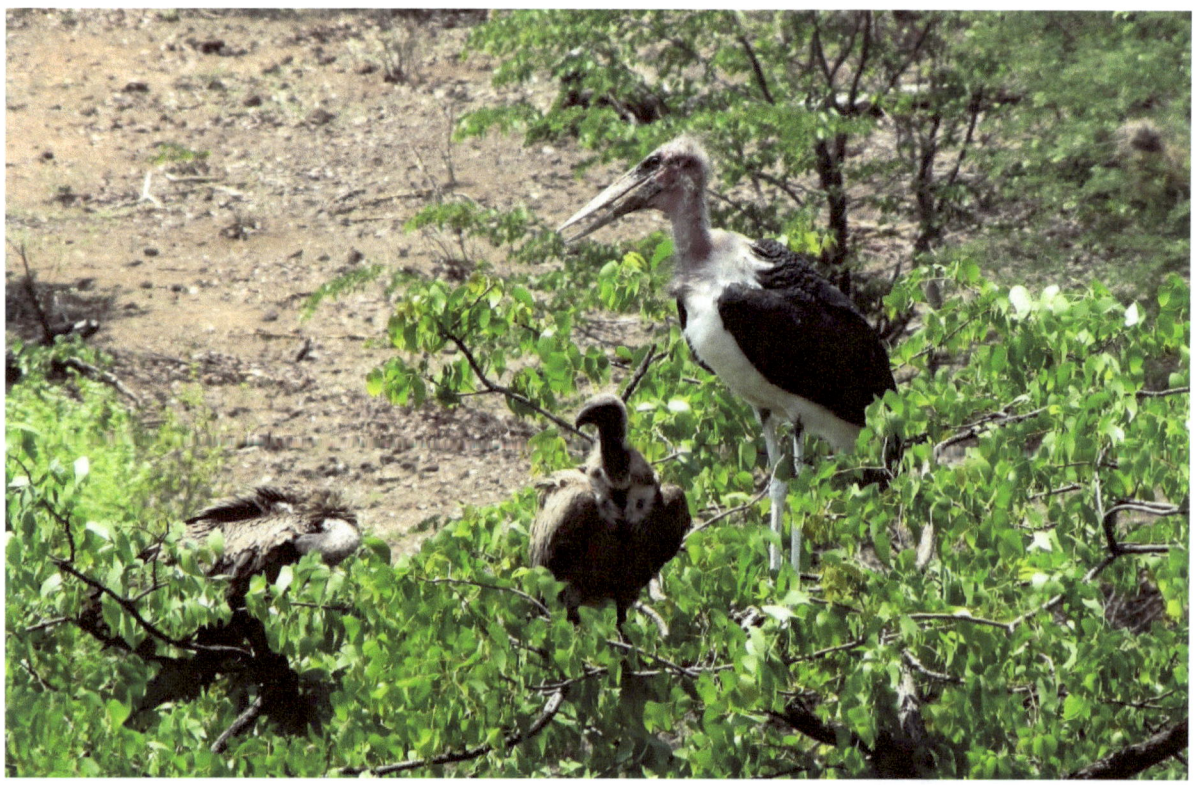

Of course, they don't look all that ugly standing next to what looks like a species of stork, akin to the marabou stork.

Feathers, Fur and Flowers

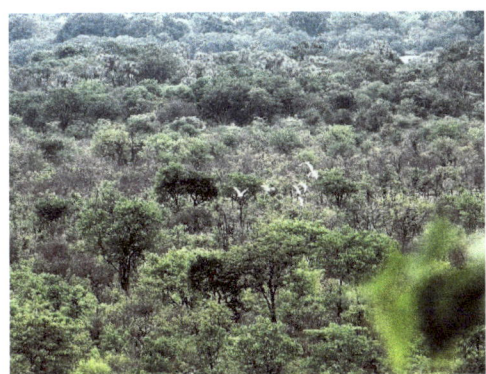 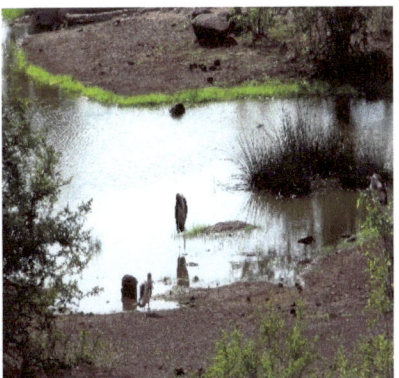

Vultures flying over the bush, and wading in a waterhole at Victoria Falls, Zimbabwe.

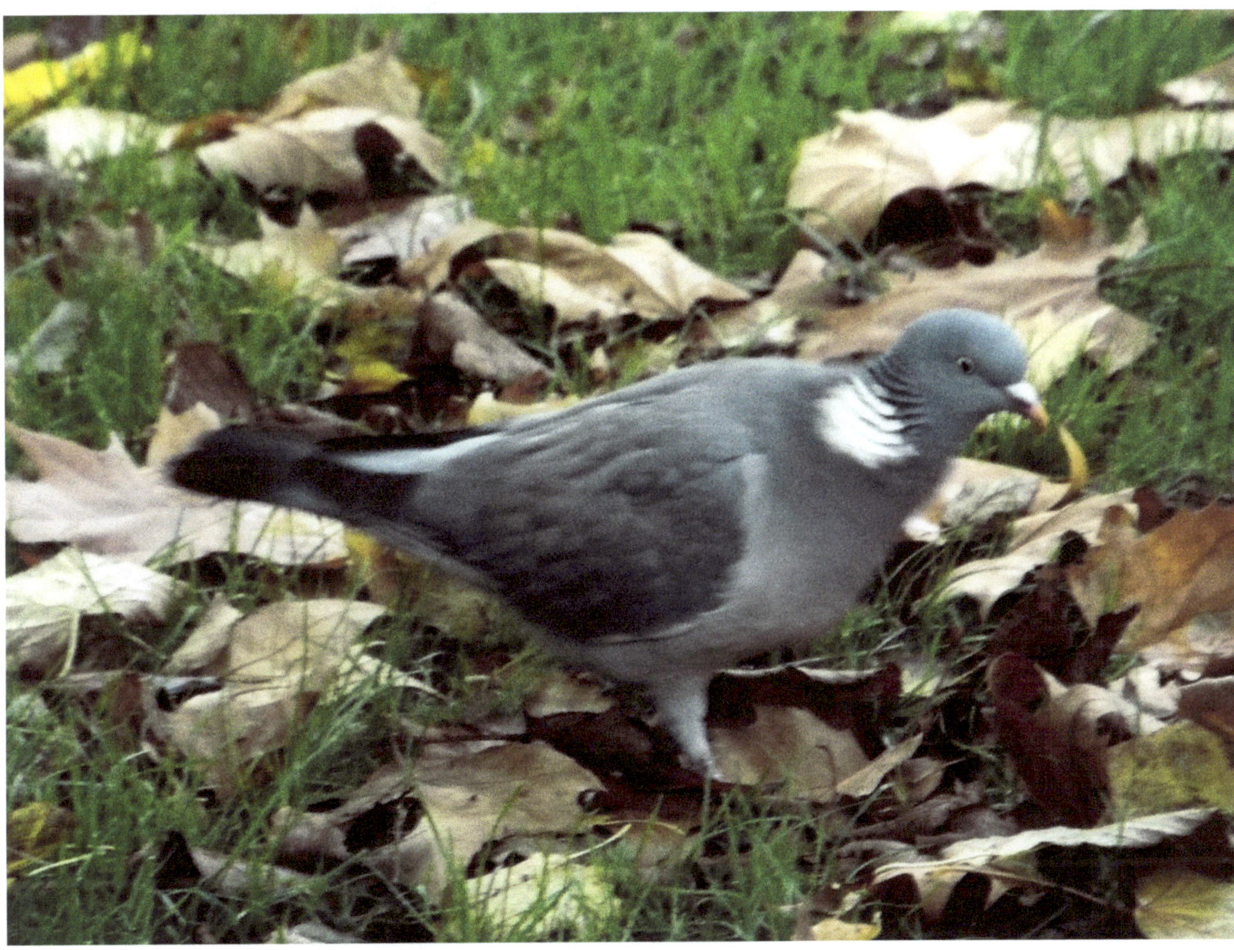

London wouldn't be London without pigeons in the park.

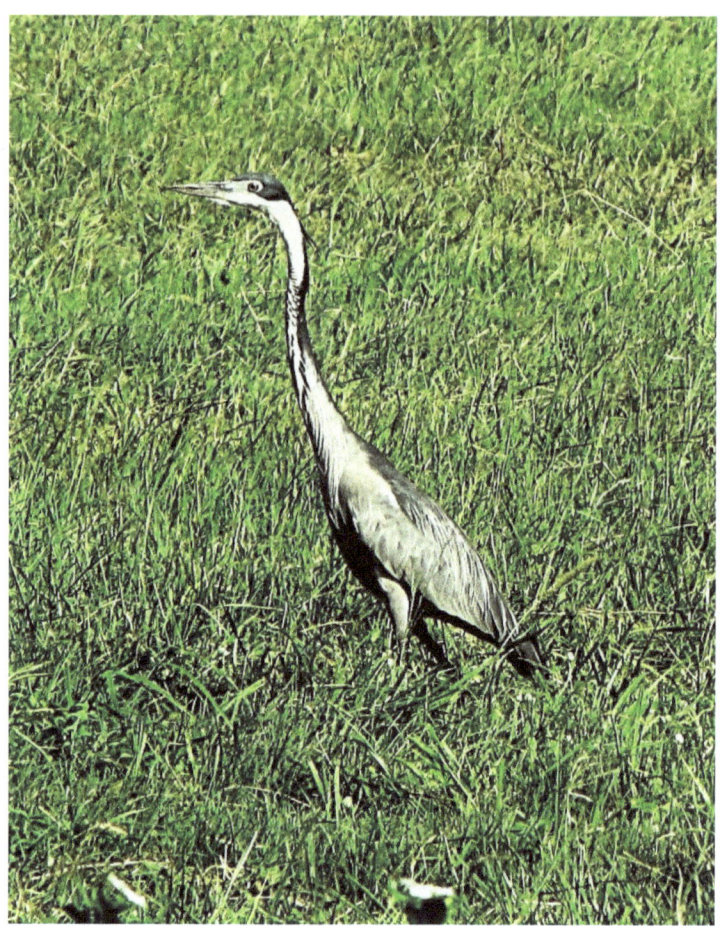

Caught sight of this one near the runway in Tanzania in the shadow of Mount Kilimanjaro.

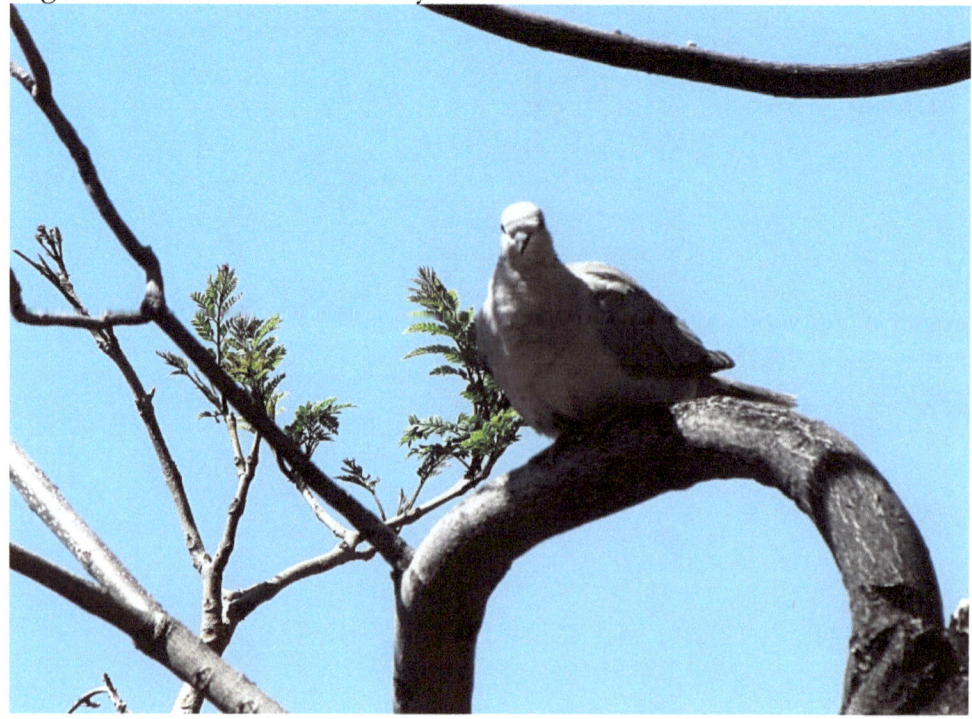

Dove on a branch outside my hotel window in Tenerife, Canary Islands.

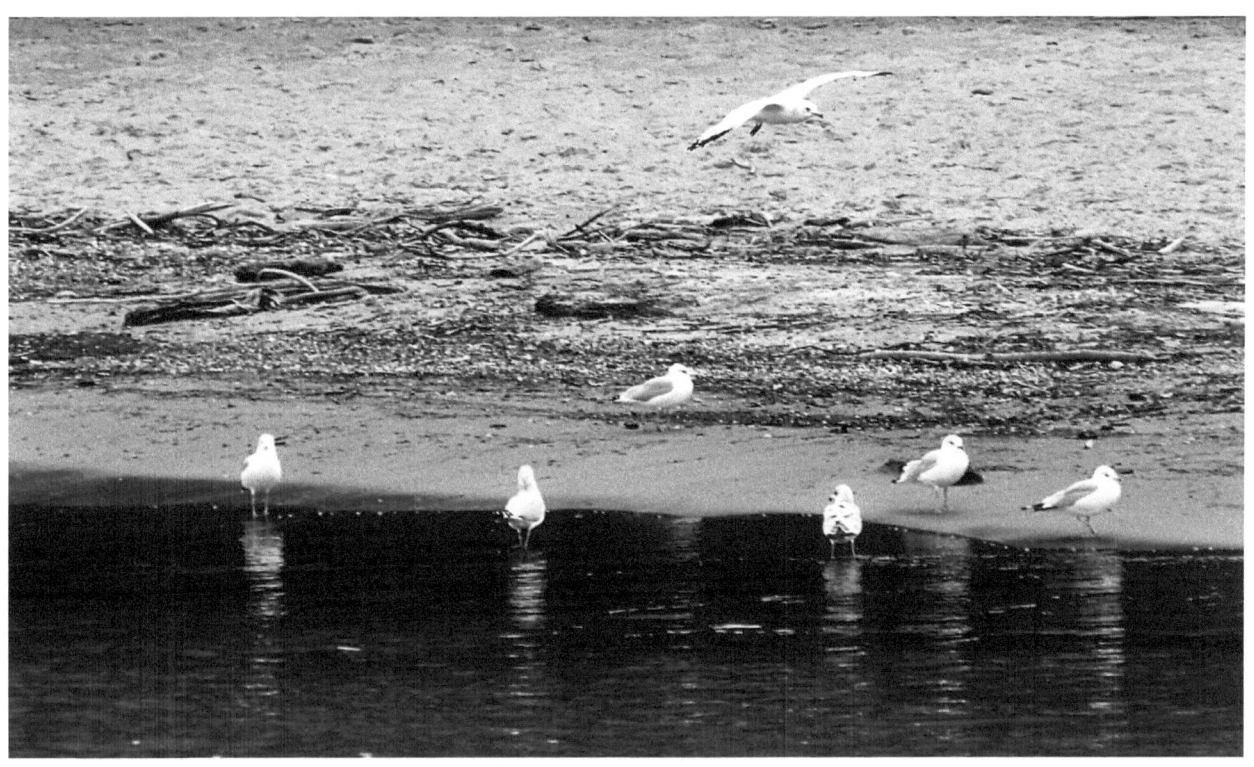

A flock of seagulls on the beach at Lake Erie, north of Chautauqua, New York.

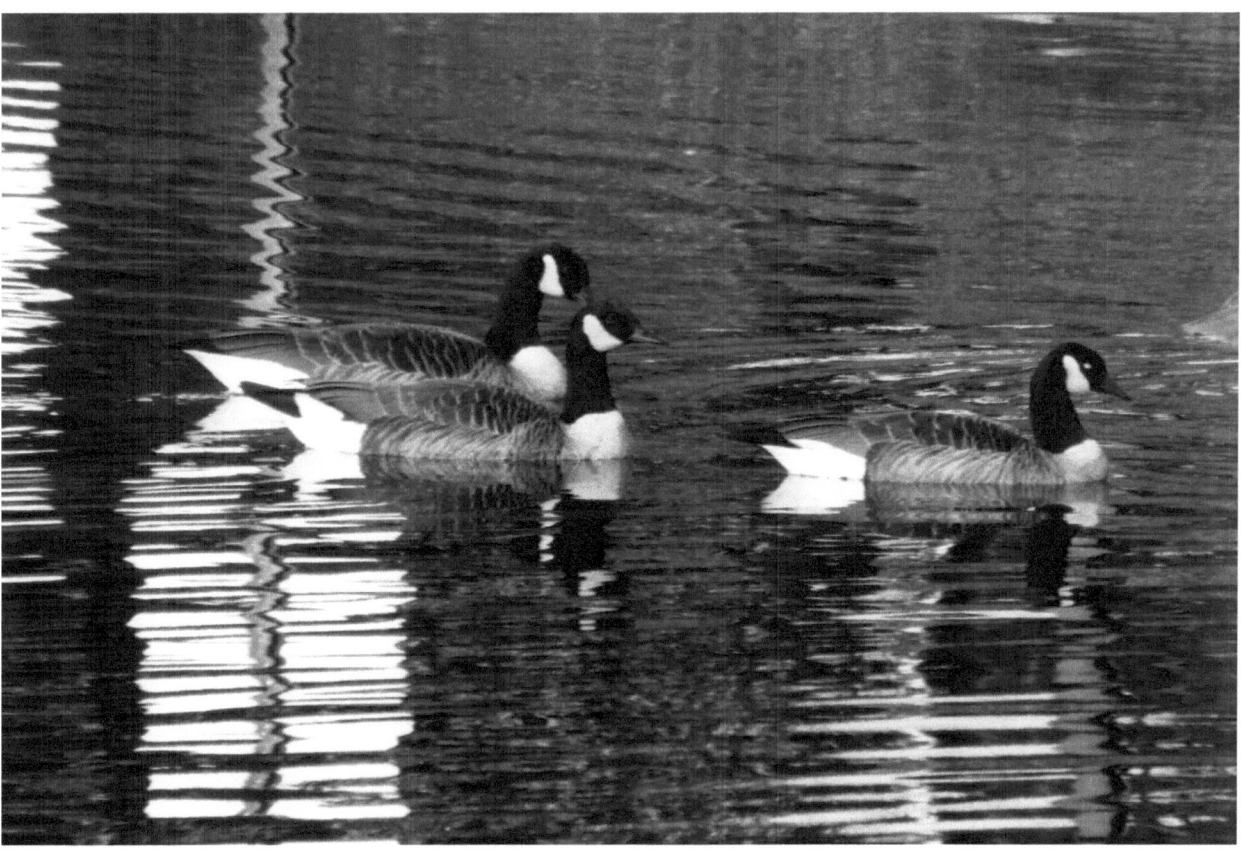

Canadian geese swimming in a pond near Gaithersburg, Maryland.

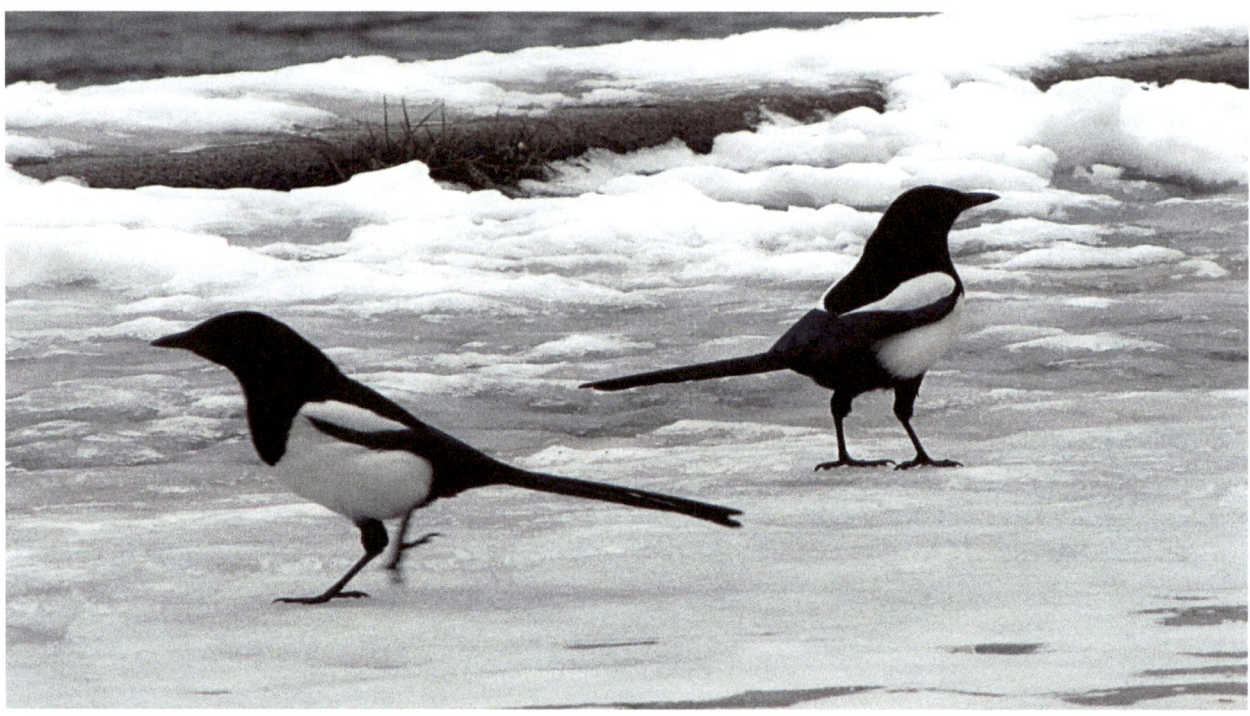

Unidentified species of bird, similar to the American crow, but with different markings. On the waterfront in Copenhagen, Denmark in winter.

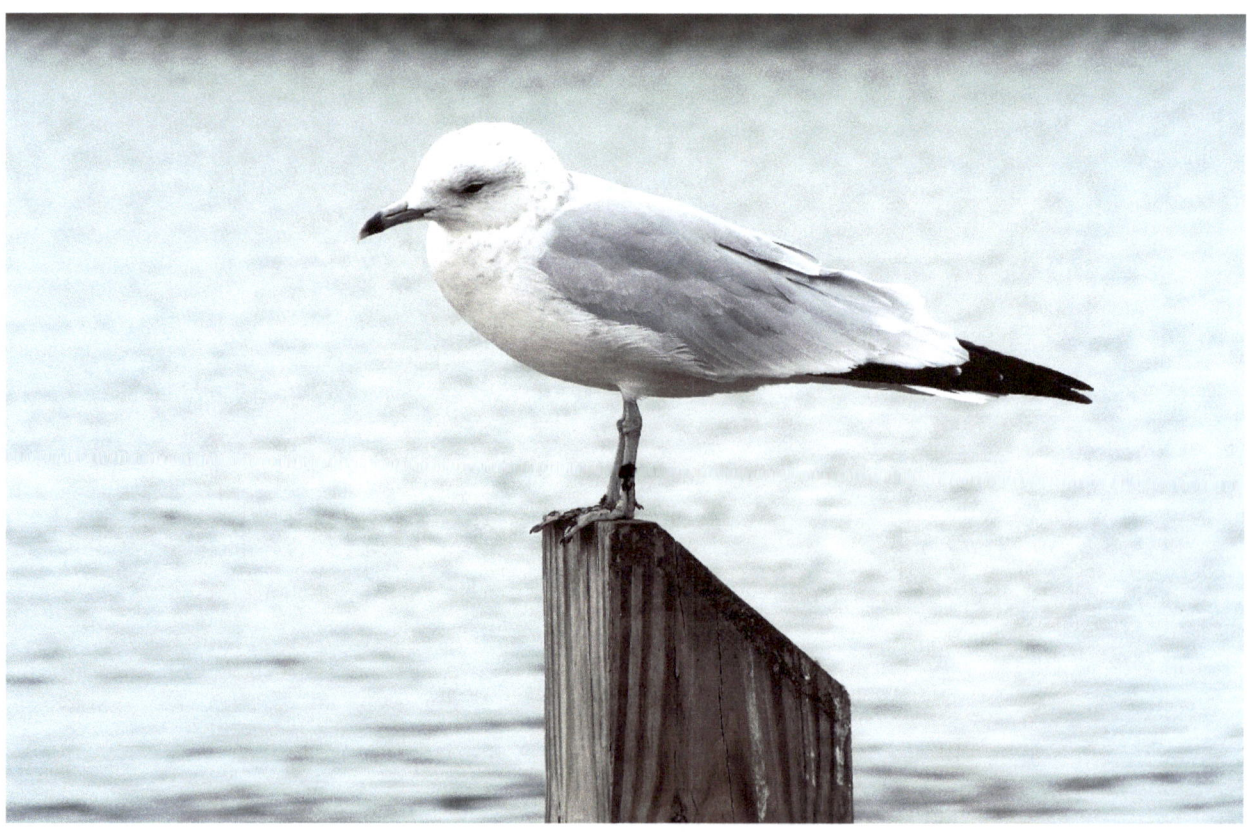

Seagull on a wharf post on Lake Erie, north of Chautauqua, New York

FUR

In the interest of full disclosure, not all the subjects of the following photographs are covered with fur. Some have a leathery hide, and a crocodile has, well, a crocodile hide; similar to a frog's only tougher. Absolute accuracy would have necessitated coming up with a new title, and I like the alliteration of the current title, so please forgive the slight inaccuracy, and enjoy the photos of animals mainly from southern Africa, but with a few from other areas, and not all of them are wild. Domesticated animals are to me as much a part of nature as those in the wild. You will no doubt notice, from the number of photos I have of lions, that, while I'm allergic to domestic cats, these big cats are one of my favorites.

I have endeavored to identify every species, but as with the birds, that's not always possible.

For the squeamish, the photos that look like extreme closeups of dangerous animals, like one looking down the gaping maw of a crocodile, were actually shot with a telephoto lens. I did on one or two occasions get fairly close to a critter who could do me great harm, like standing thirty yards from a bull rhino protecting his cow and calf—which is, of course, the one I'm leading with—or walking with a pair of lion cubs in Antelope Park in Zimbabwe.

I once stood under a tree limb around which a six-foot black snake had wrapped itself. Fortunately, black snakes are relatively harmless and nonpoisonous, and this one had just eaten, so no real danger there.

I don't recommend anyone do some of the things I've done. I was a paratrooper, and I think I bumped my head one time too many on bad landings. You should never approach a dangerous animal, especially one with young. That's what telephoto lenses are for.

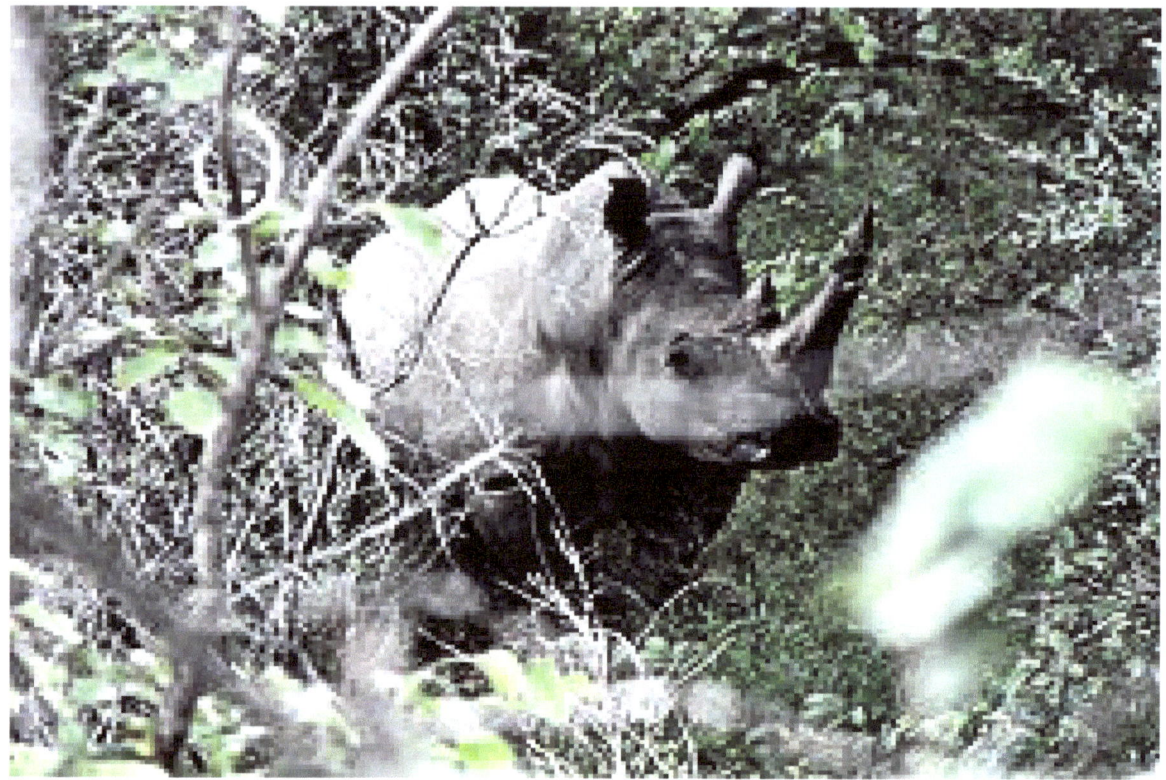

On foot patrol with the park rangers at Matobo National Park, in Zimbabwe, I came within thirty yards of this bull rhino.

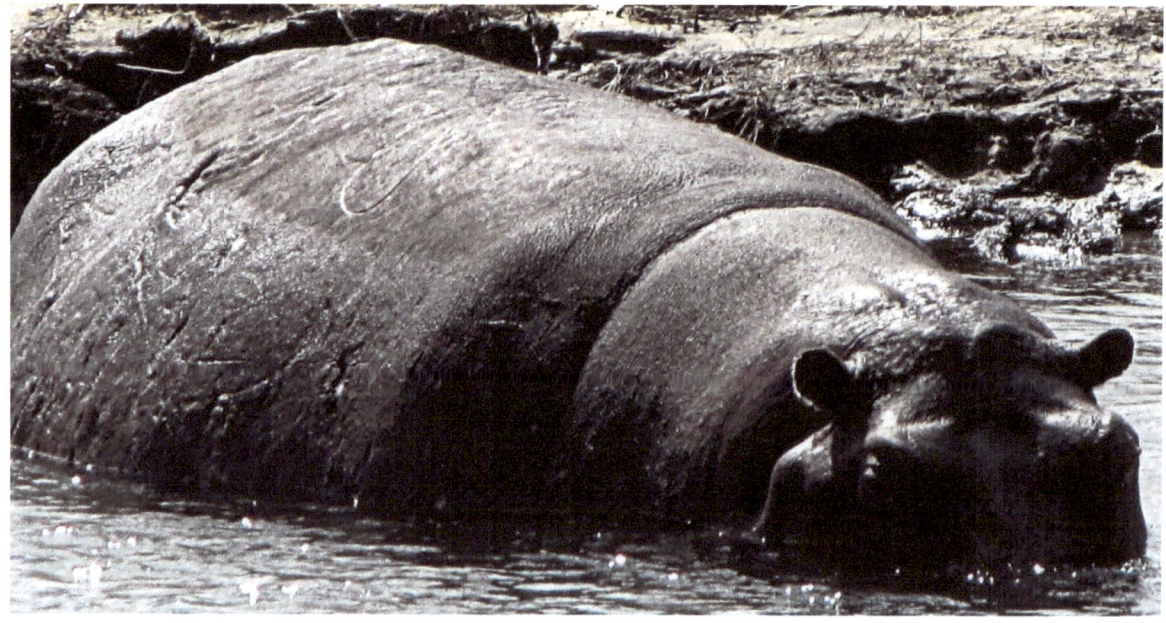

Another risky shot. I was walking along the banks of the Zambezi River at Mano Pools in Zimbabwe, when I saw this hippo watching me from the water.

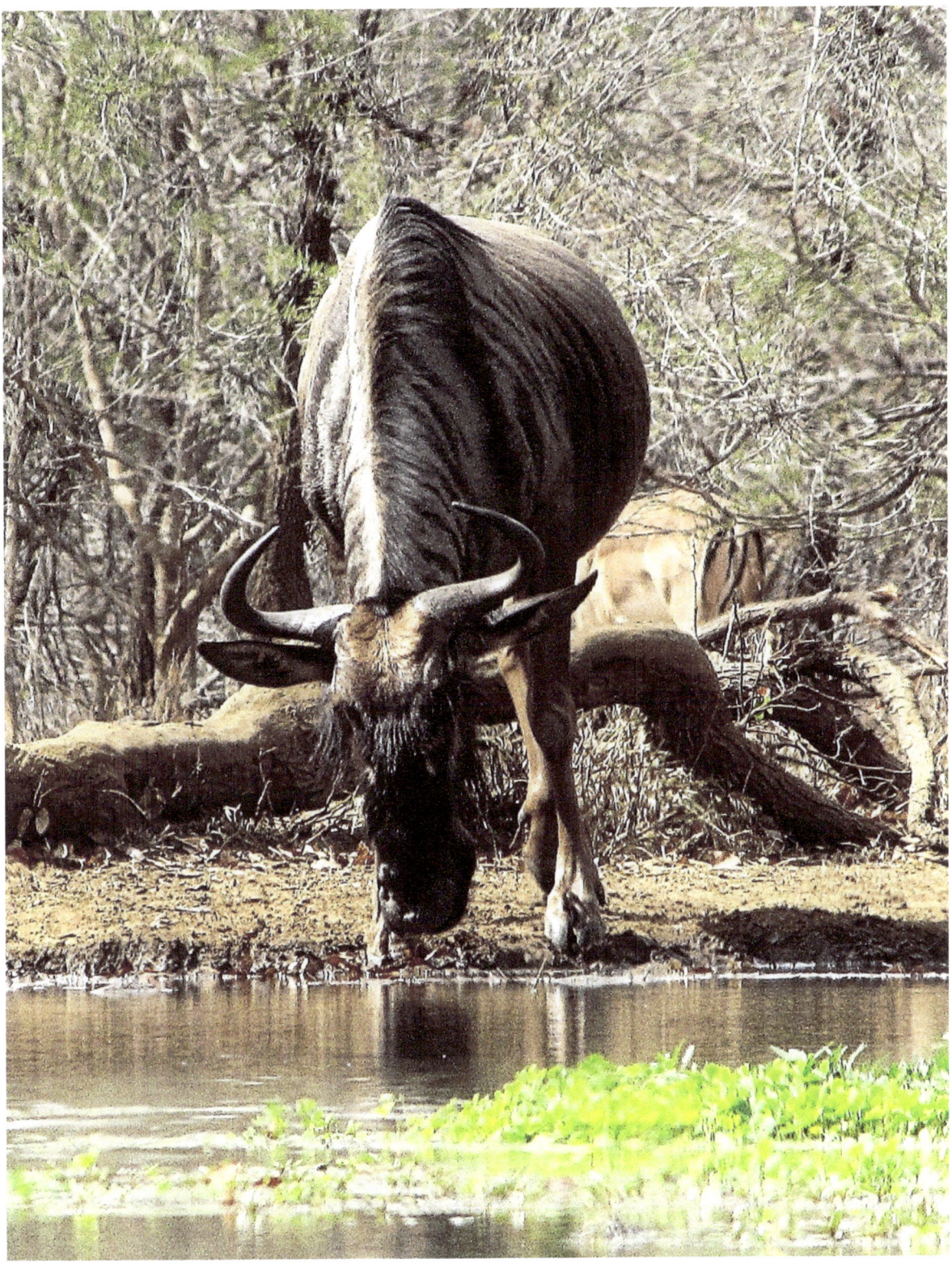

A wildebeest drinking from a water hole in southeastern Zimbabwe.

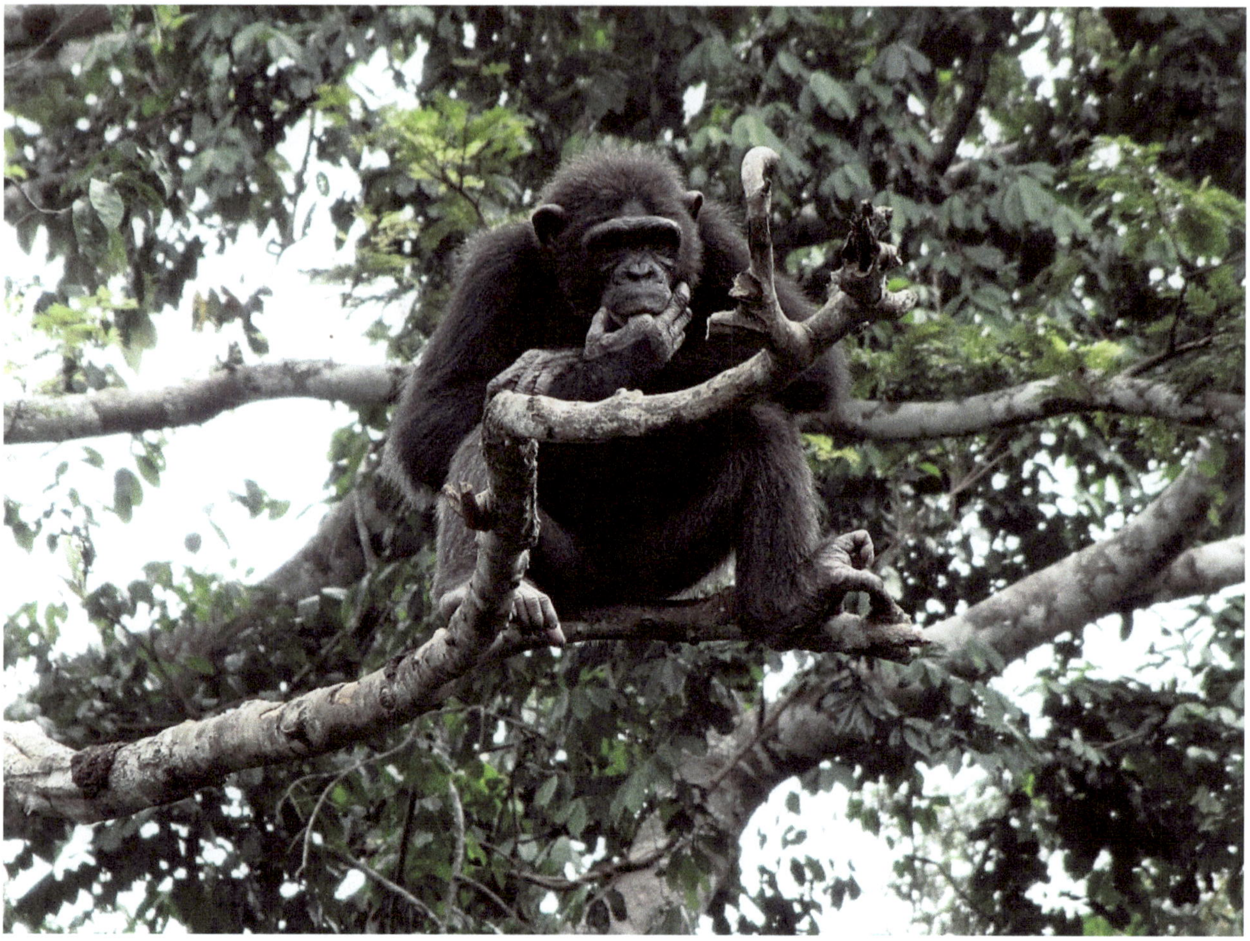

A chimpanzee in Cameroon.

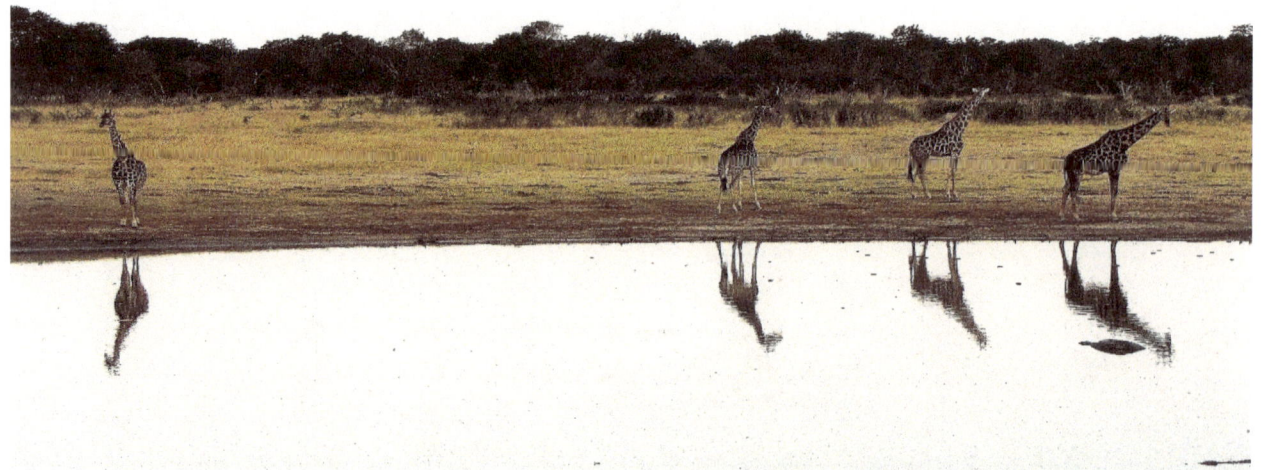

Giraffes at a water hole in Hwange, Zimbabwe.

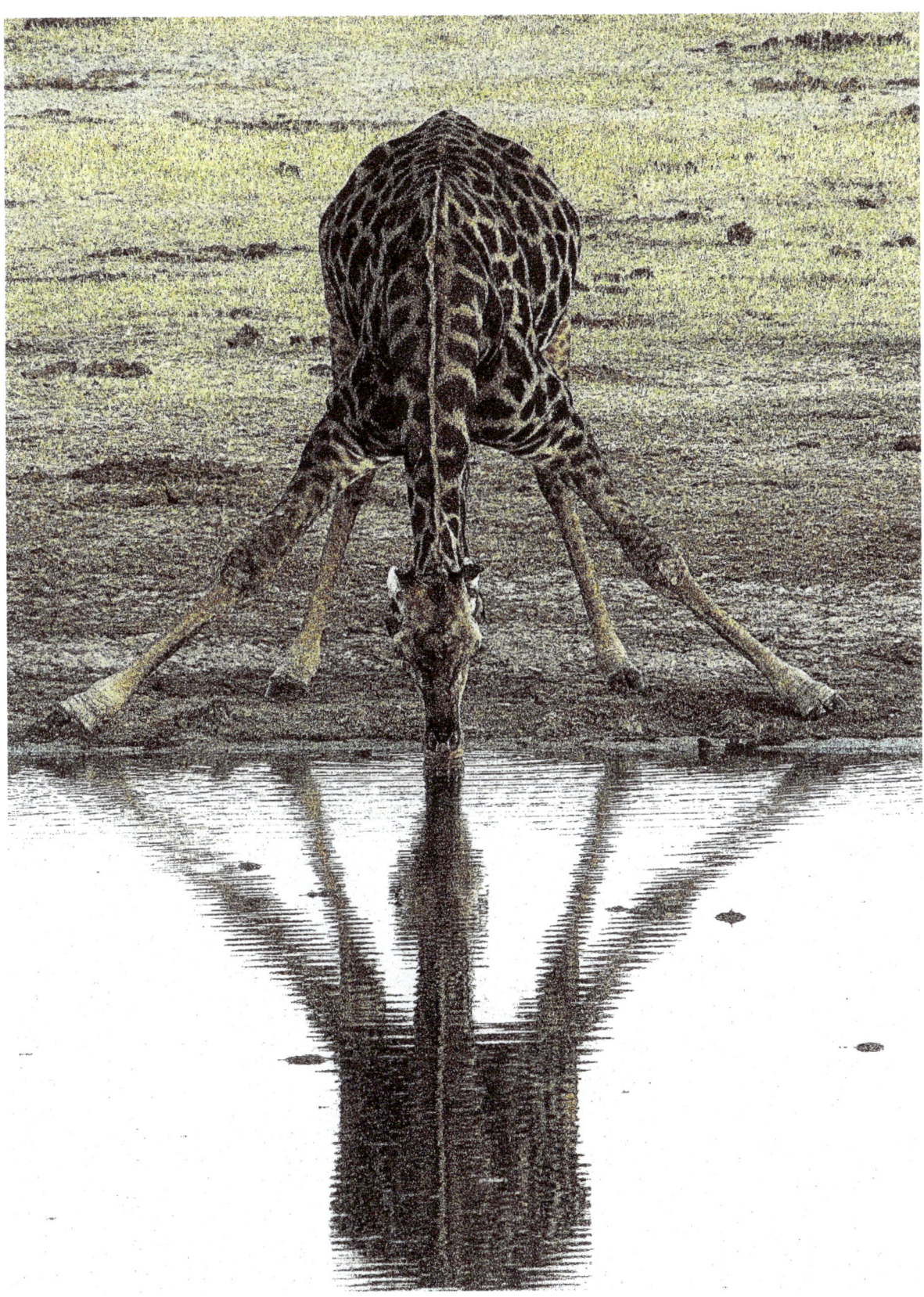

What a giraffe has to do to get a drink of water is amazing, and looks a bit uncomfortable.

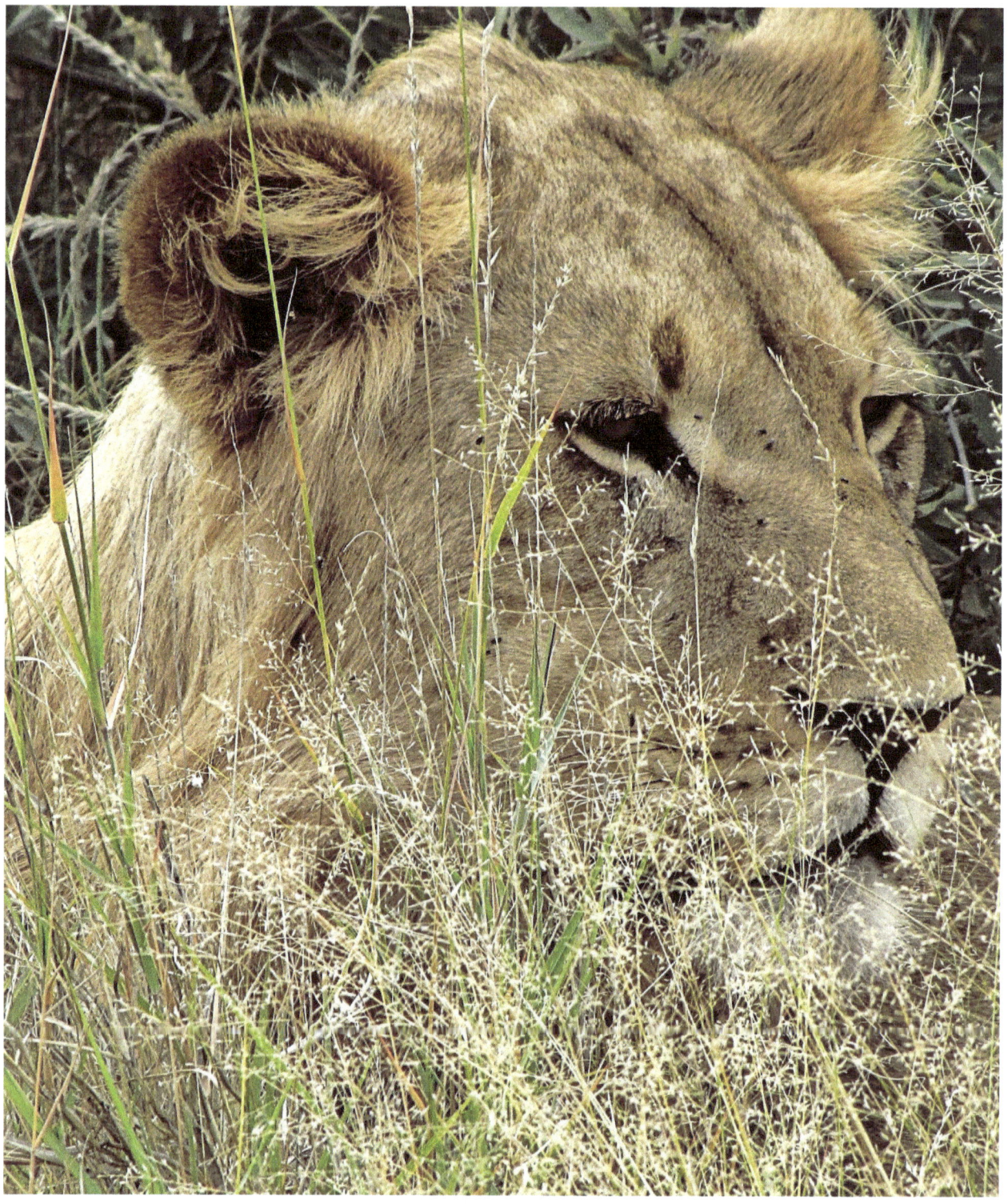

I'm fascinated by the big cats, and lions were all over southern Africa, so there are a lot of photos of lions, like this one of a young lion in the Kalahari Desert in South Africa.

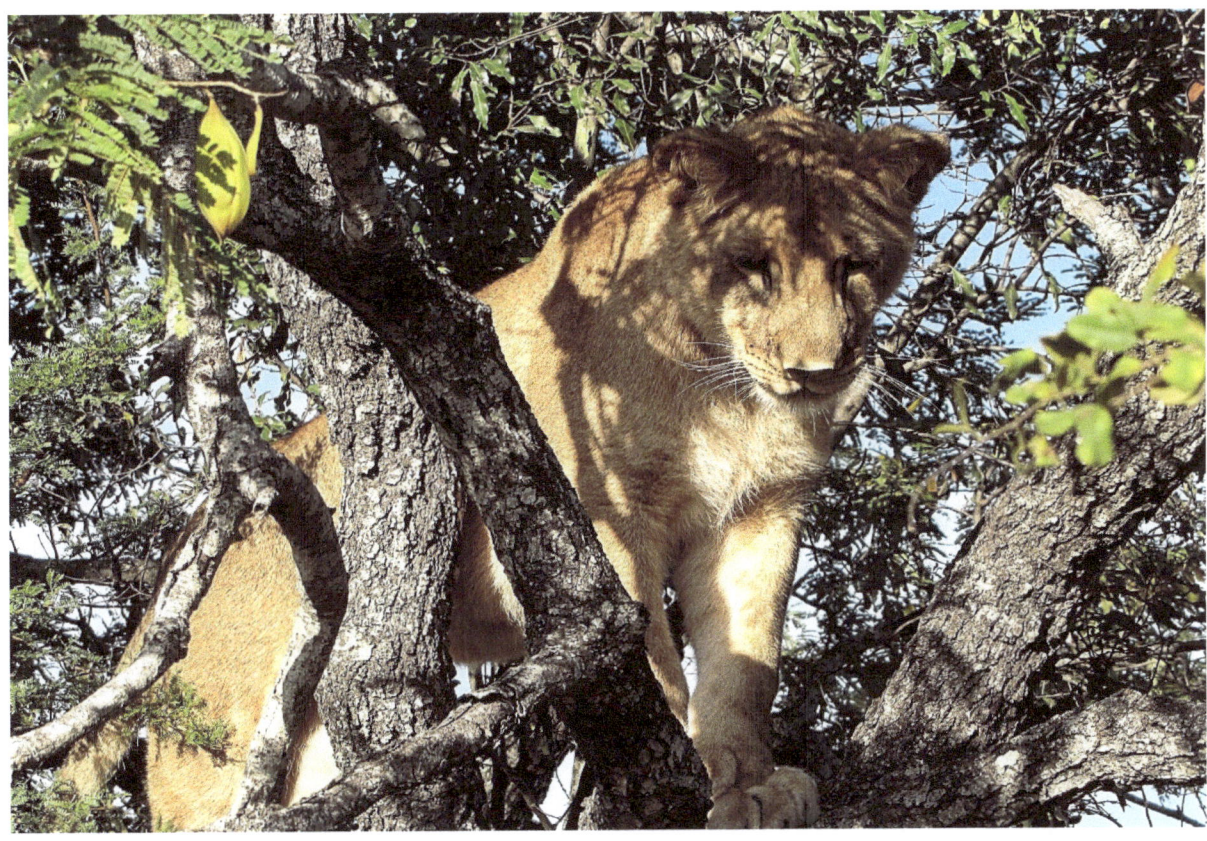

I read somewhere that lions were the only cats that couldn't climb trees. Well, this photo of a lion in a tree in Antelope Park, Zimbabwe proves that wrong.

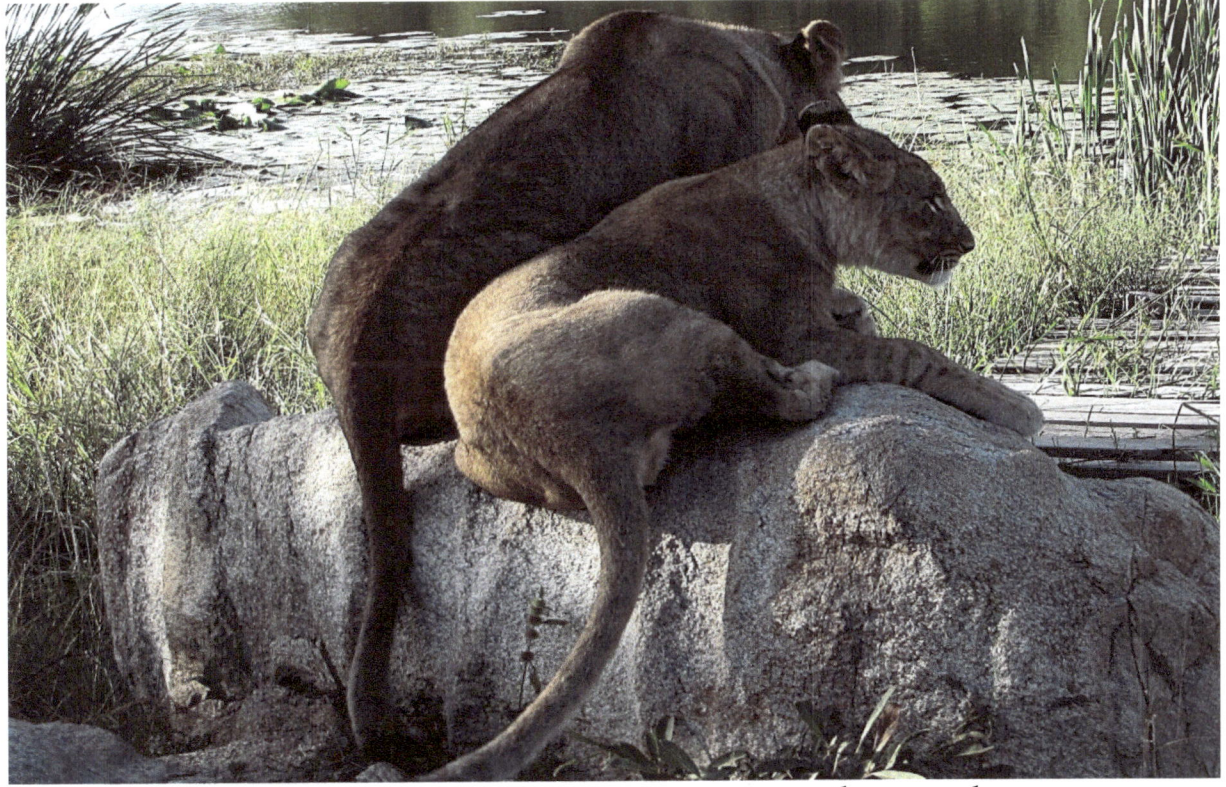

They also climb on rocks. Same venue as the one above.

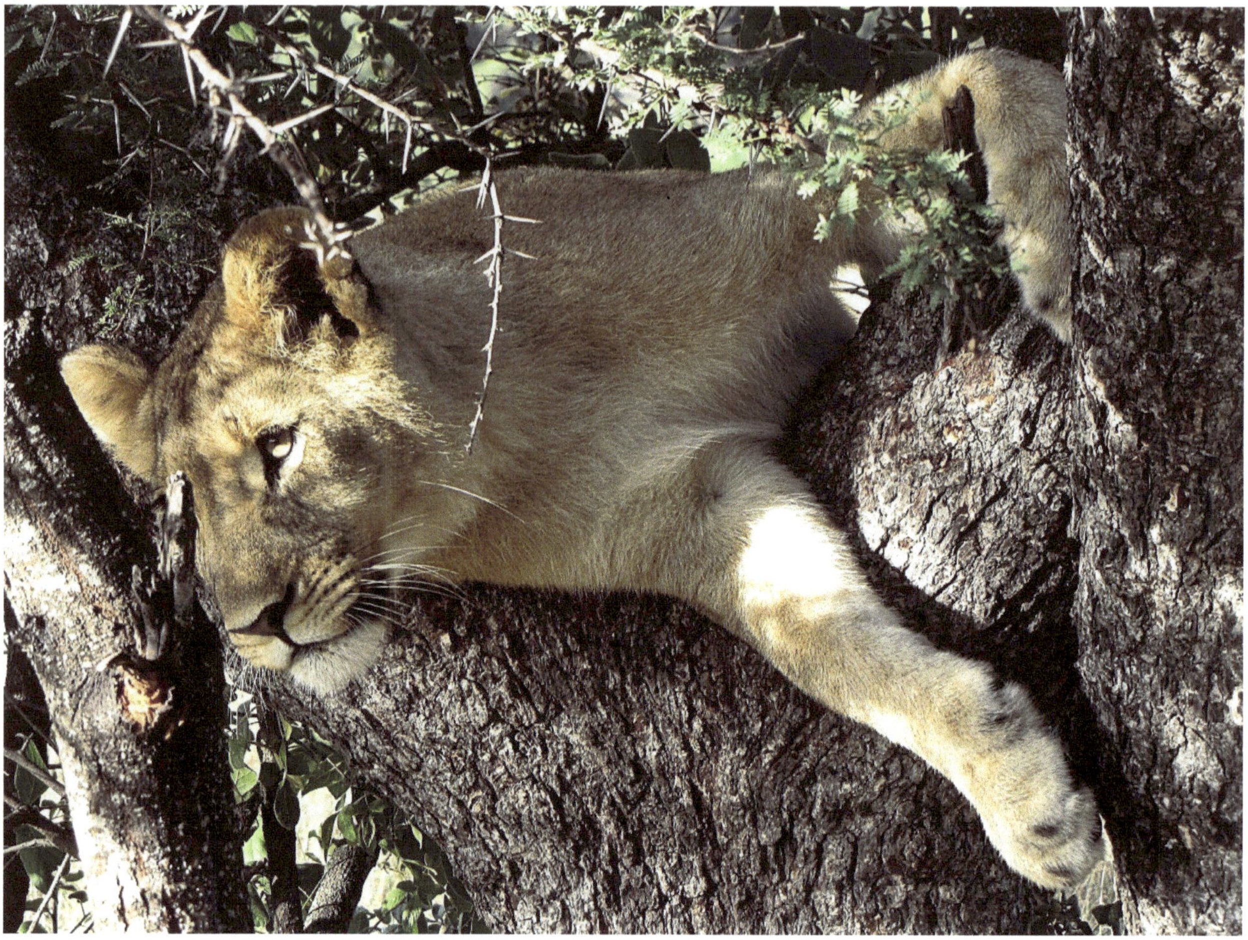

Except for the fact that she weighs over a hundred pounds, and has teeth bigger than my thumb, she looks like any old pussy cat lolling on a limb, don't you think.

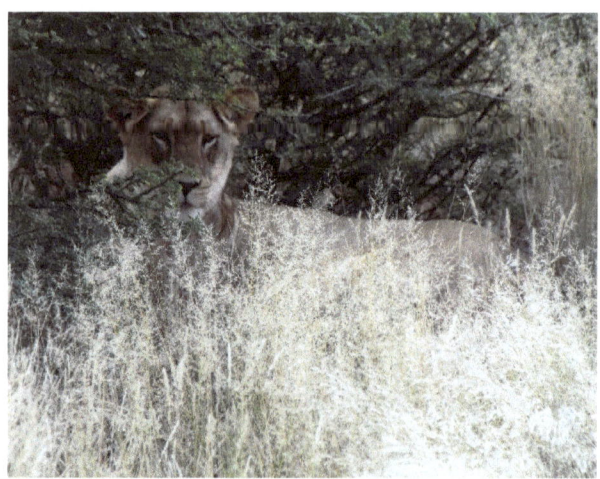
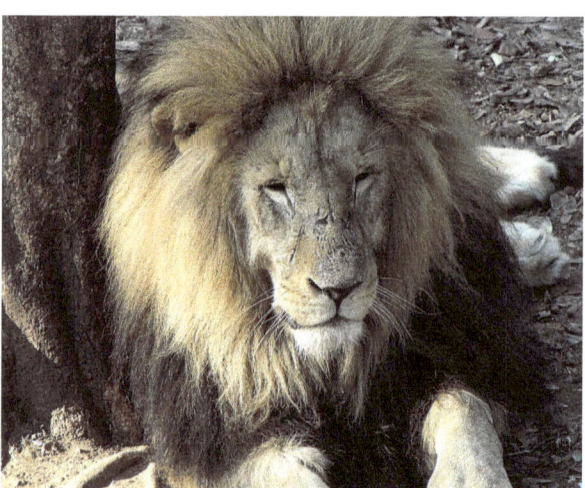

On the left, a female lion resting in thorn bushes in South Africa's Kalahari Desert, and on the right, an elderly male lion in Hwange, Zimbabwe.

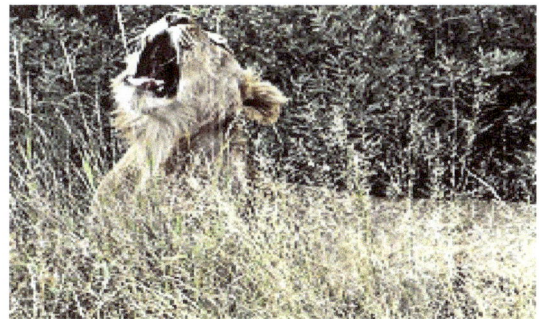 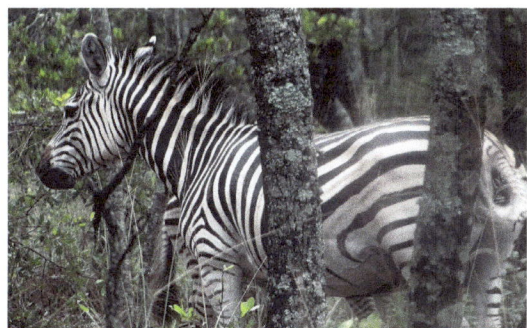

A young mail lion in the grass of the Kalahari (left) and a zebra in the bush in southeastern Zimbabwe.

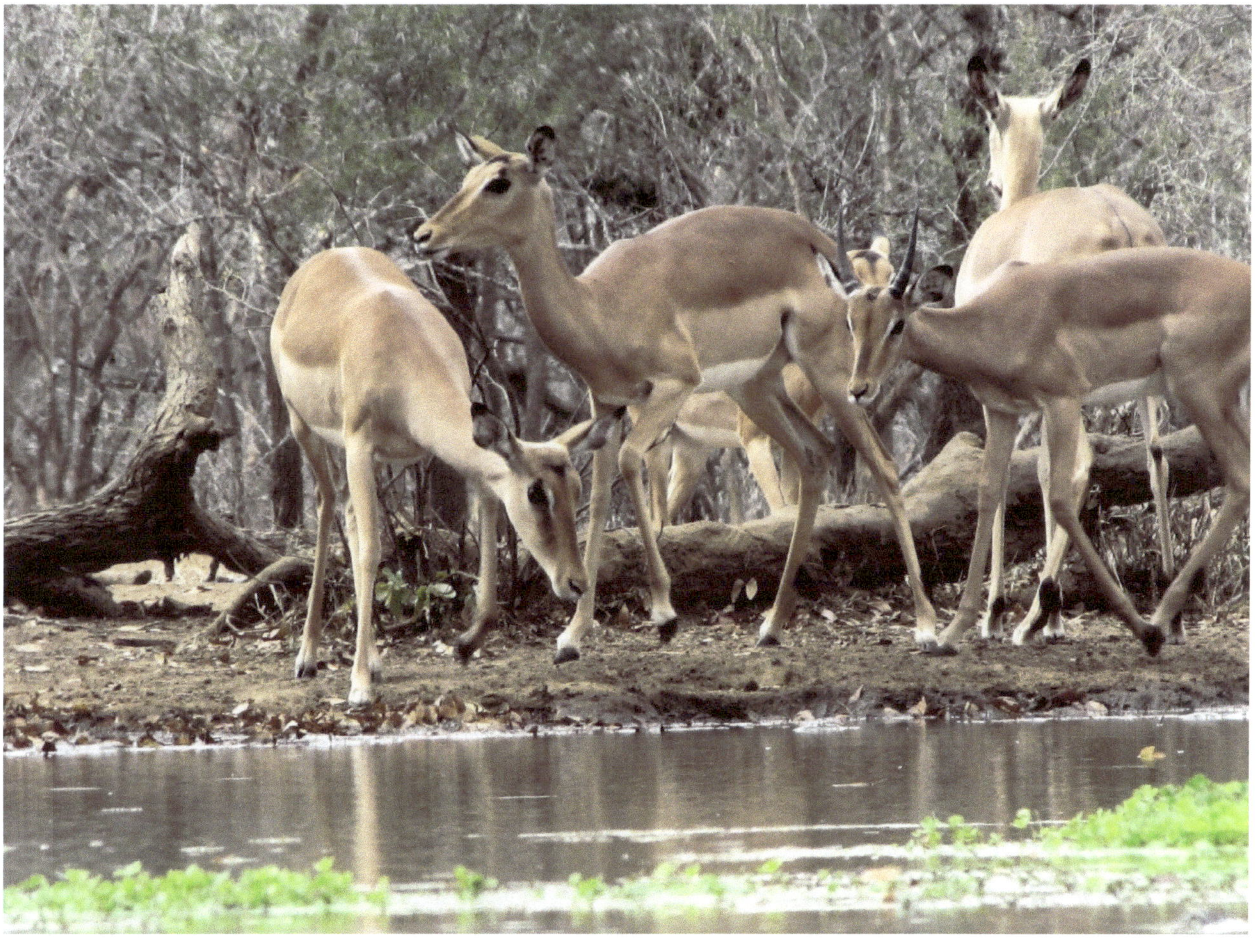

A herd of impala at a water hole in southeastern Zimbabwe.

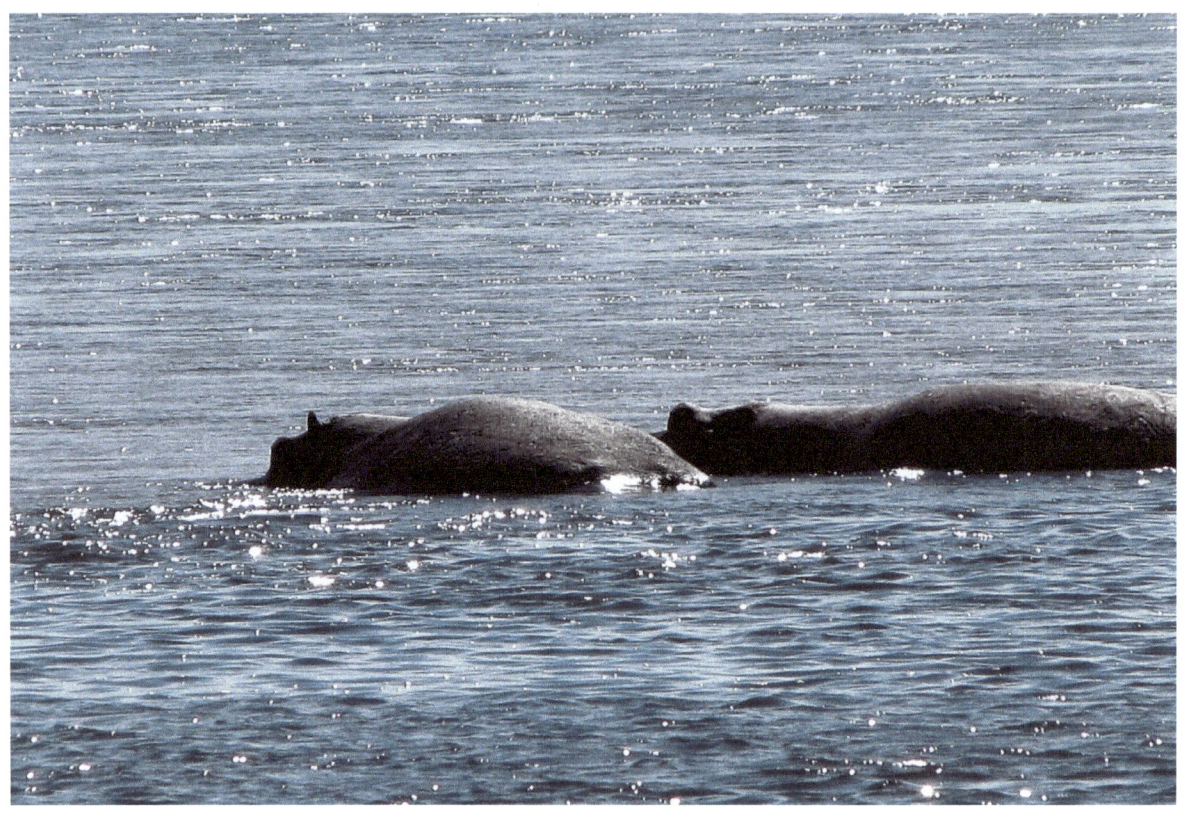

Two hippos bathing in the Zambezi River, Zimbabwe.

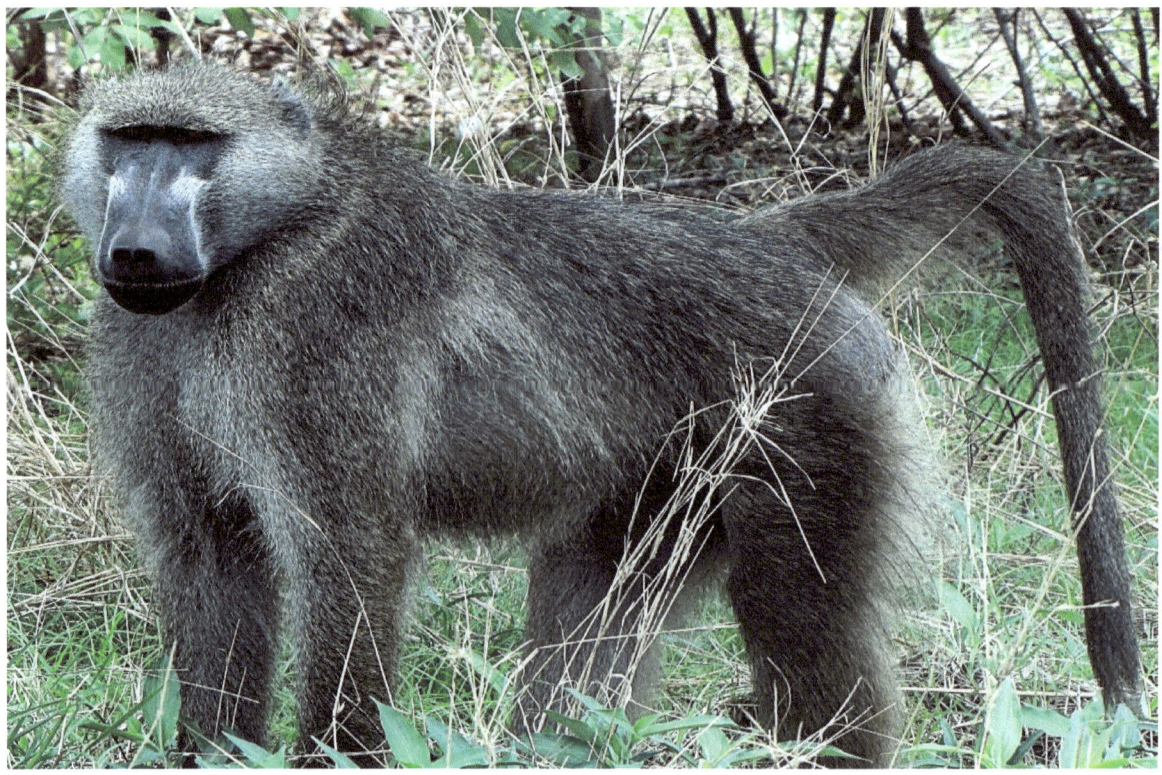

A baboon in Victoria Falls, Zimbabwe.

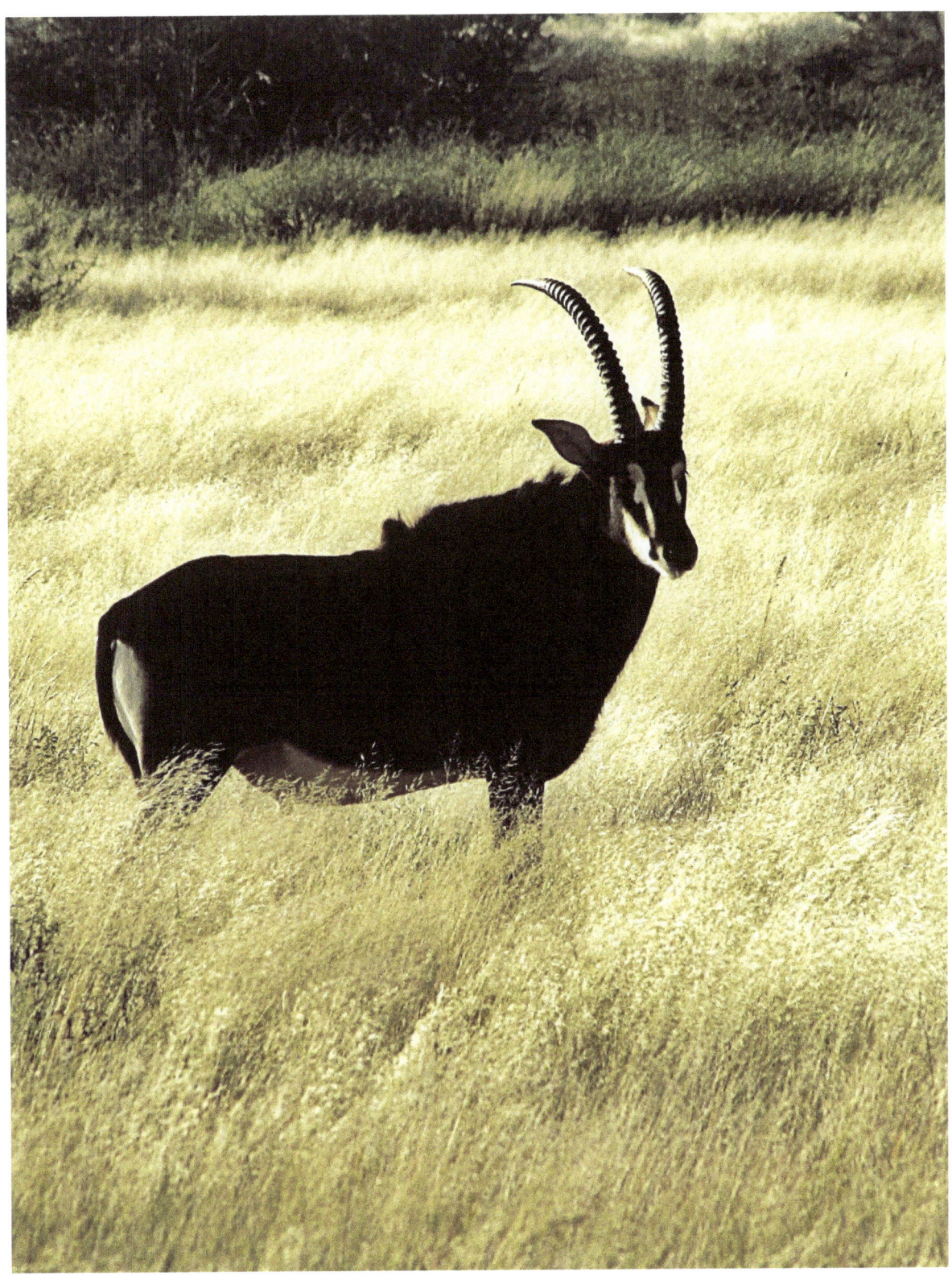

A sable antelope in South Africa's Kalahari Desert.

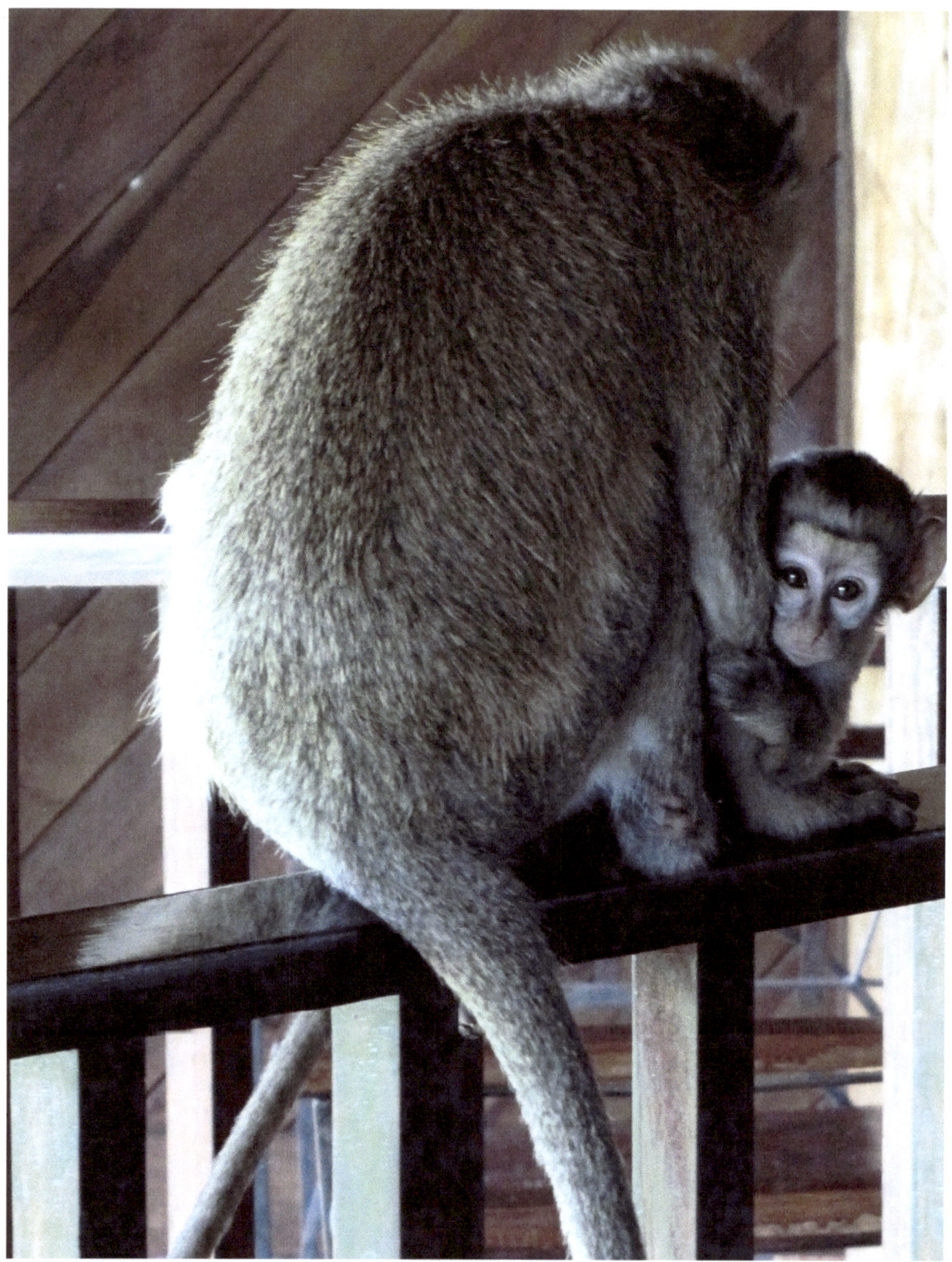

A female Vervet monkey and her baby on my hotel balcony in Victoria Falls, Zimbabwe.

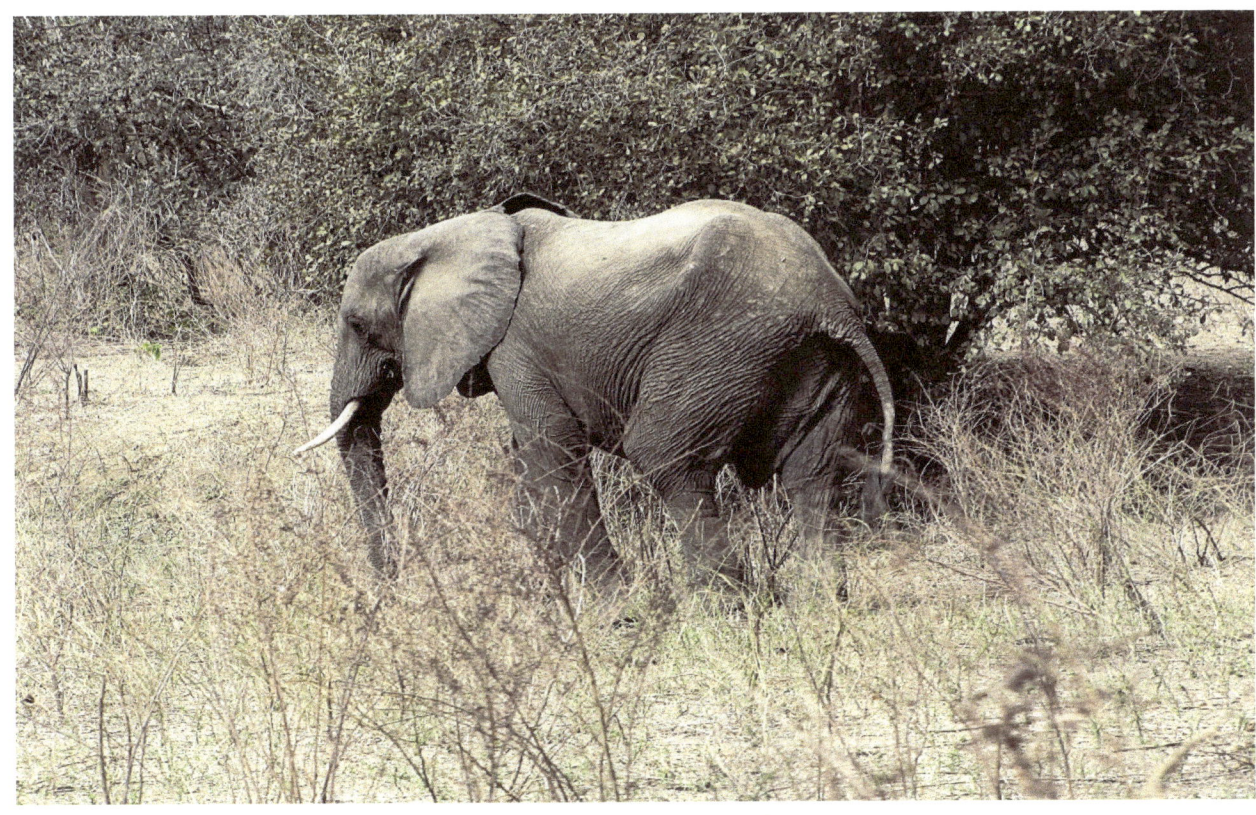

An elephant foraging in Mana Pools in Zimbabwe.

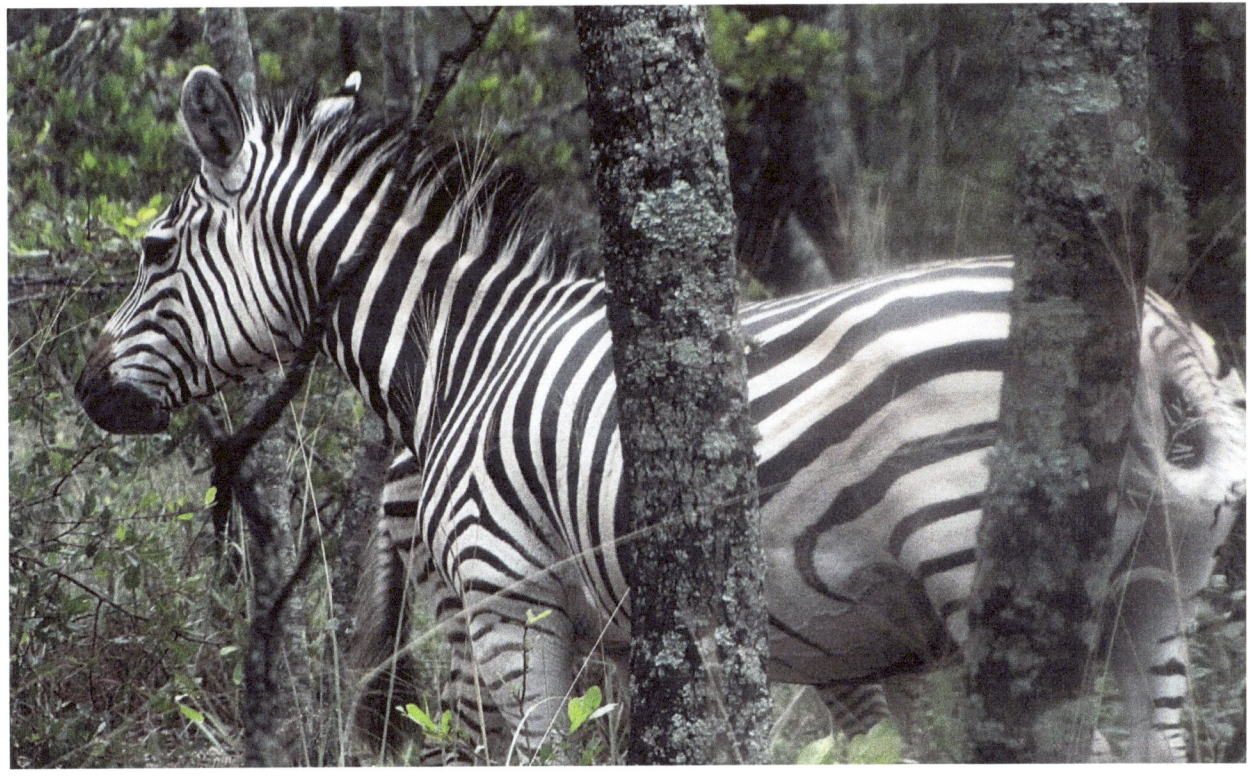

Zebra in southeast Zimbabwe.

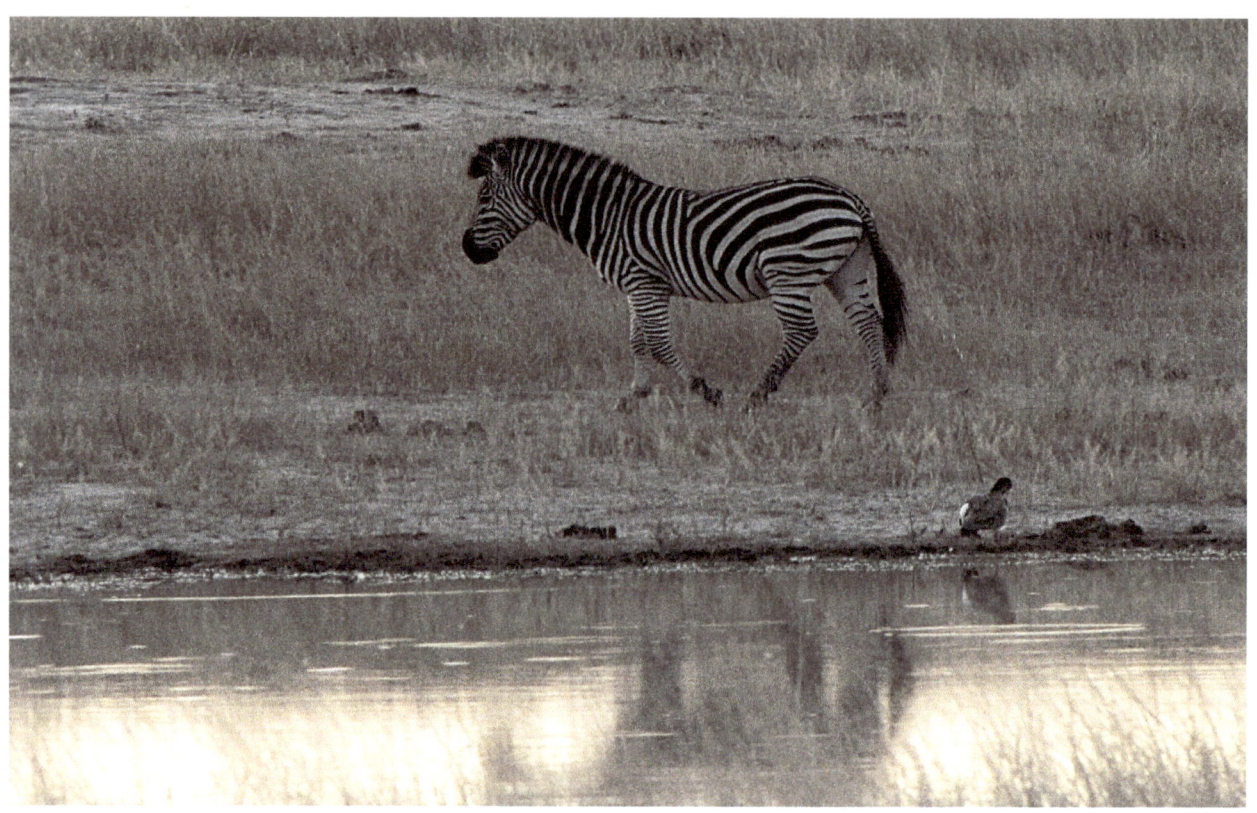
Zebra and bird at water hole in Hwange, Zimbabwe.

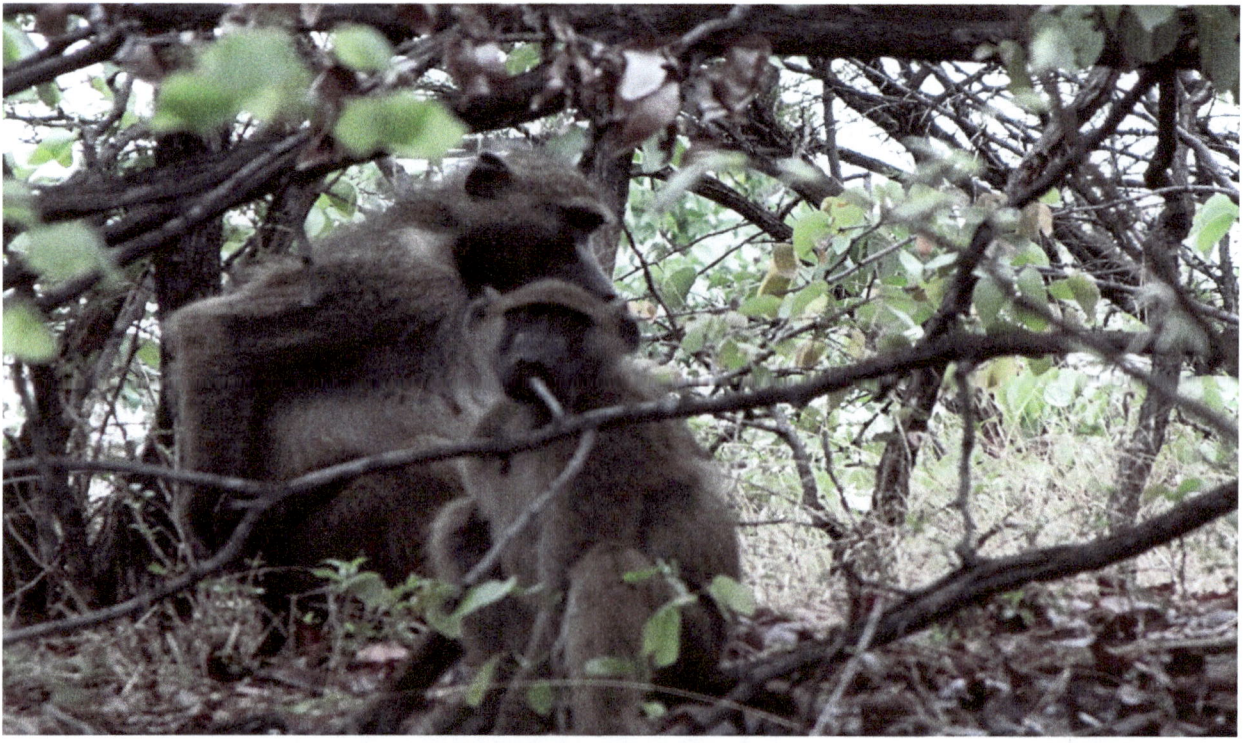
Baboon and her young one at Victoria Falls, Zimbabwe.

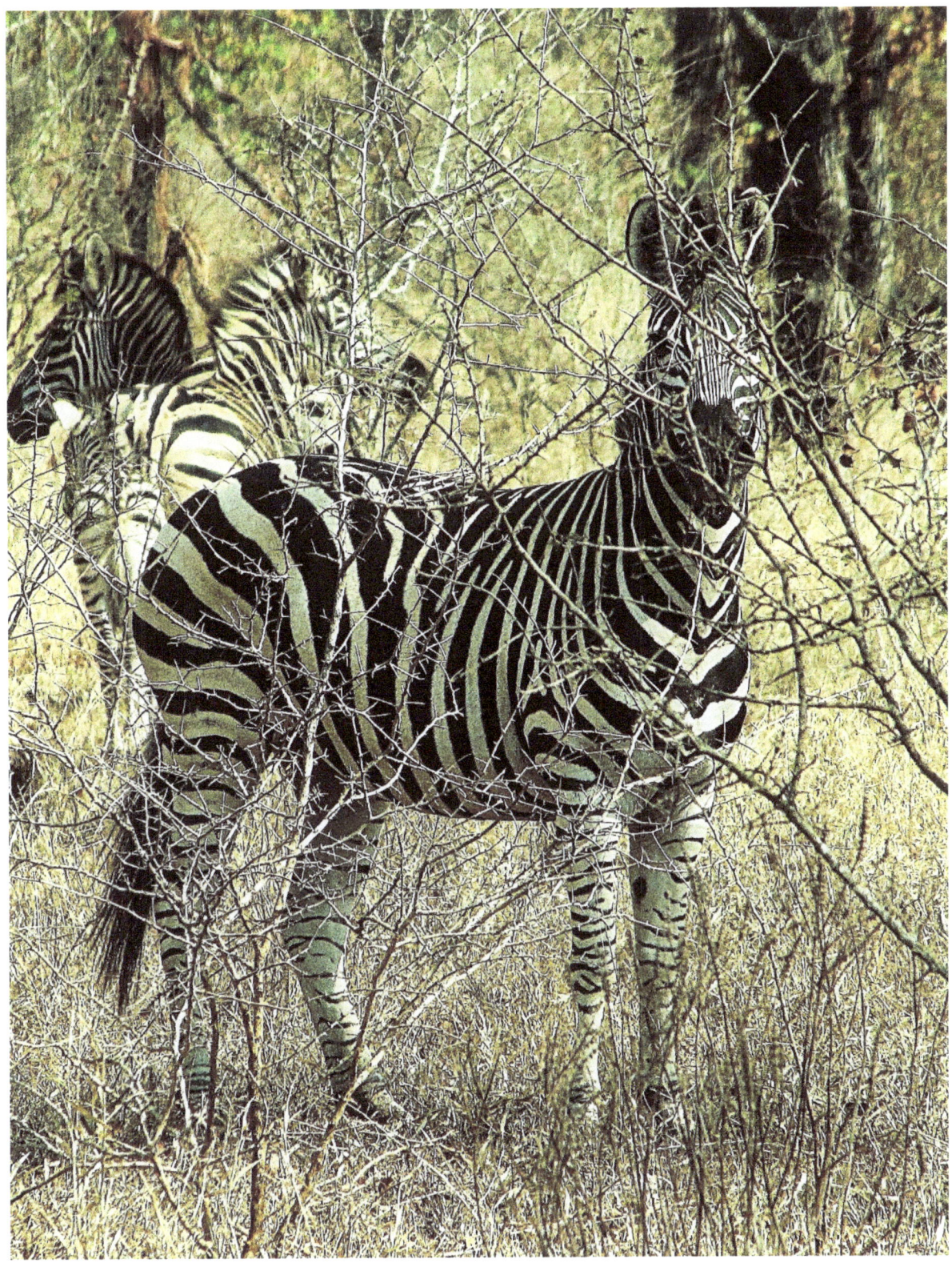

Herd of zebras in southeast Zimbabwe.

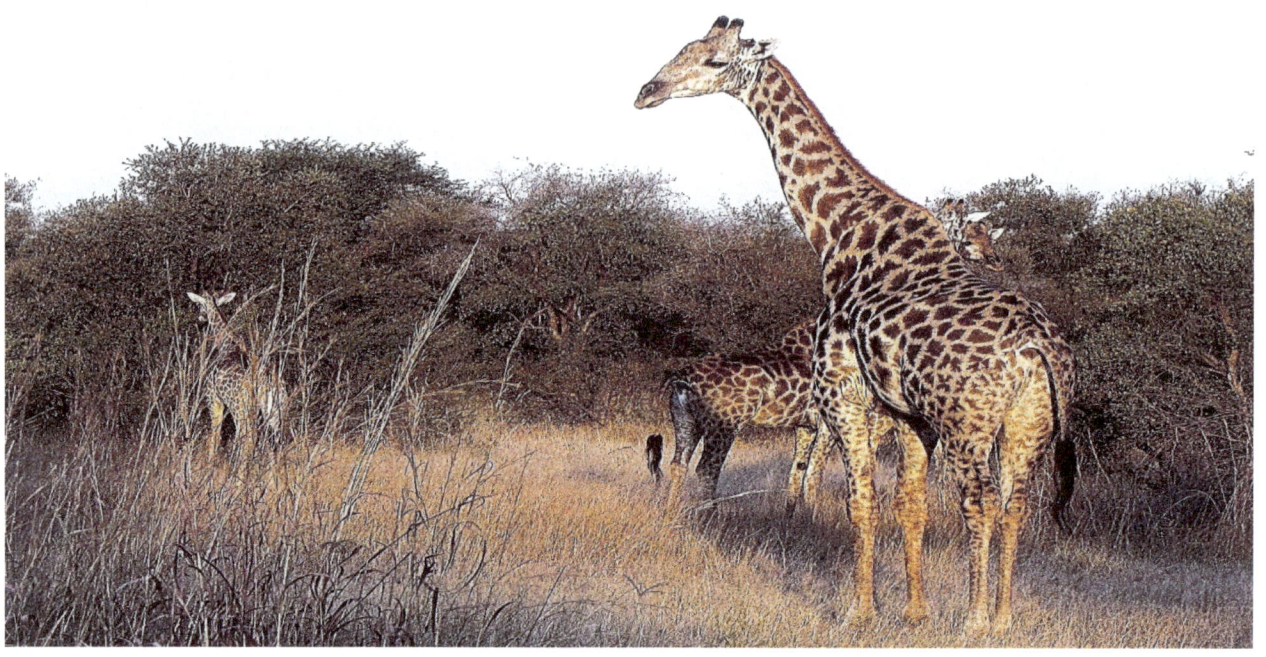
Giraffes in a game park just north of Harare, Zimbabwe.

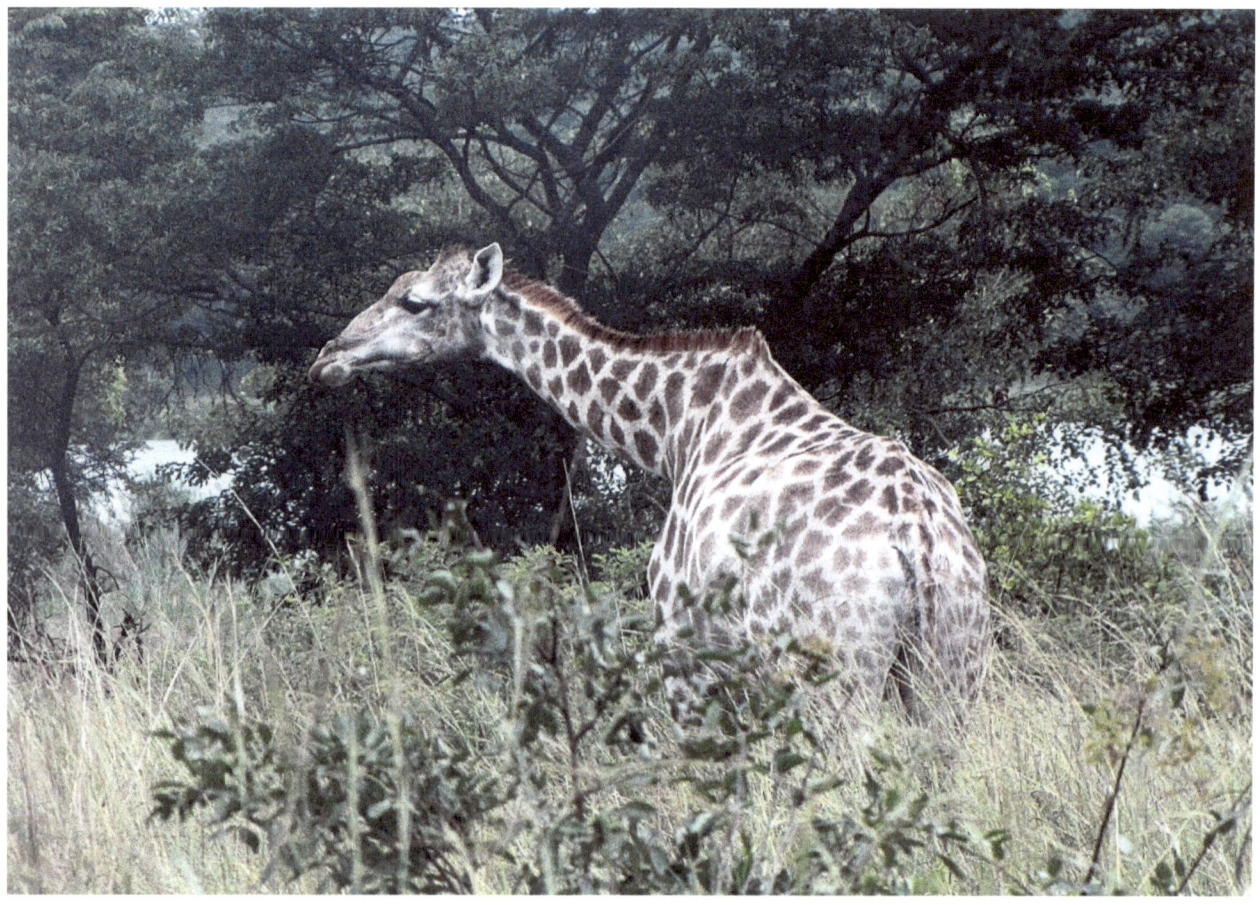
Giraffe in the brush near Hwange, Zimbabwe.

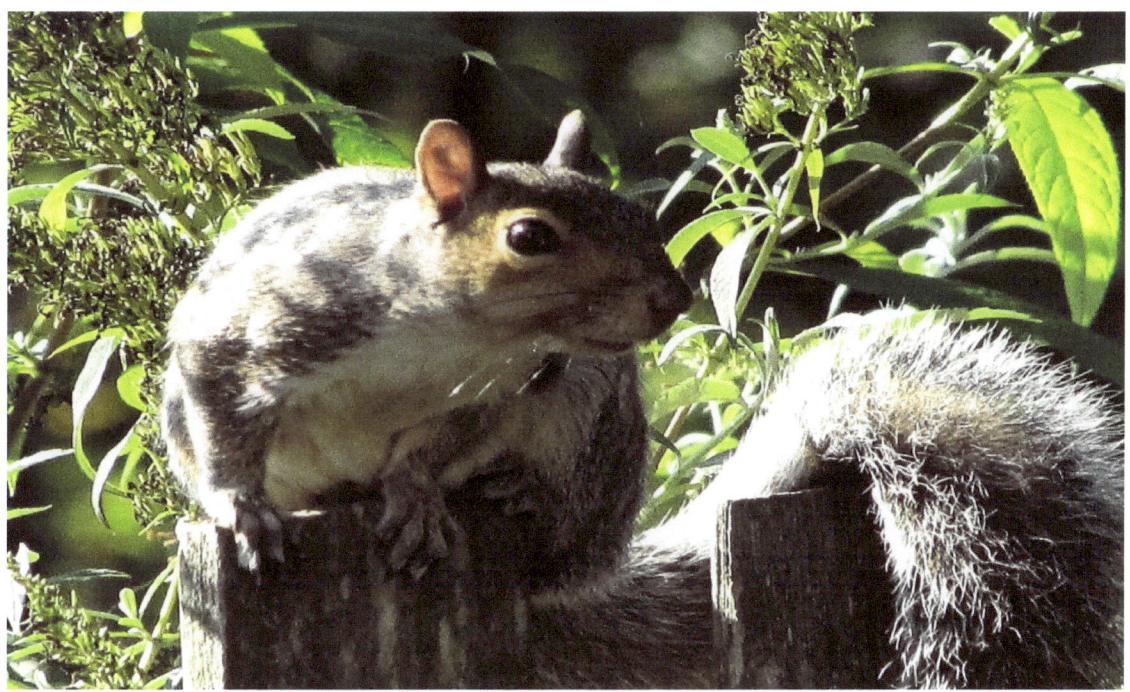

This squirrel was on the fence in my backyard in Maryland.

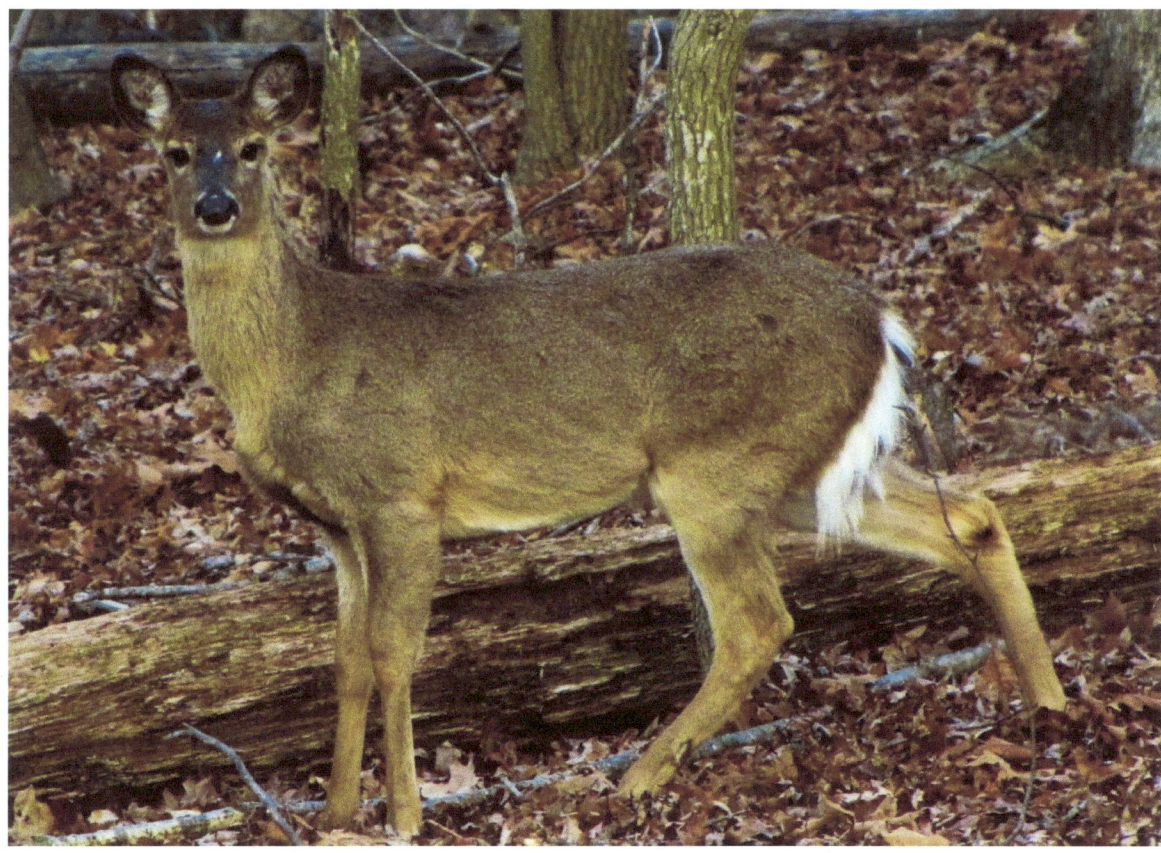

This deer was grazing in my backyard in Maryland, which you can see is forested.

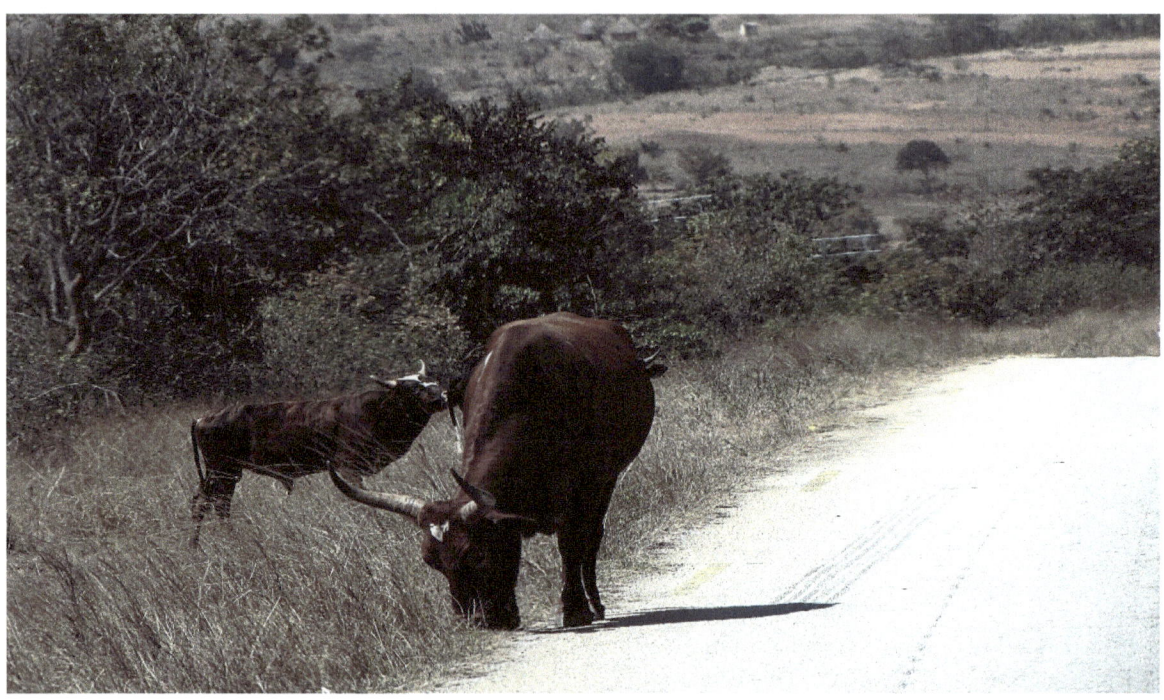

Cattle grazing along the road in northeastern Zimbabwe.

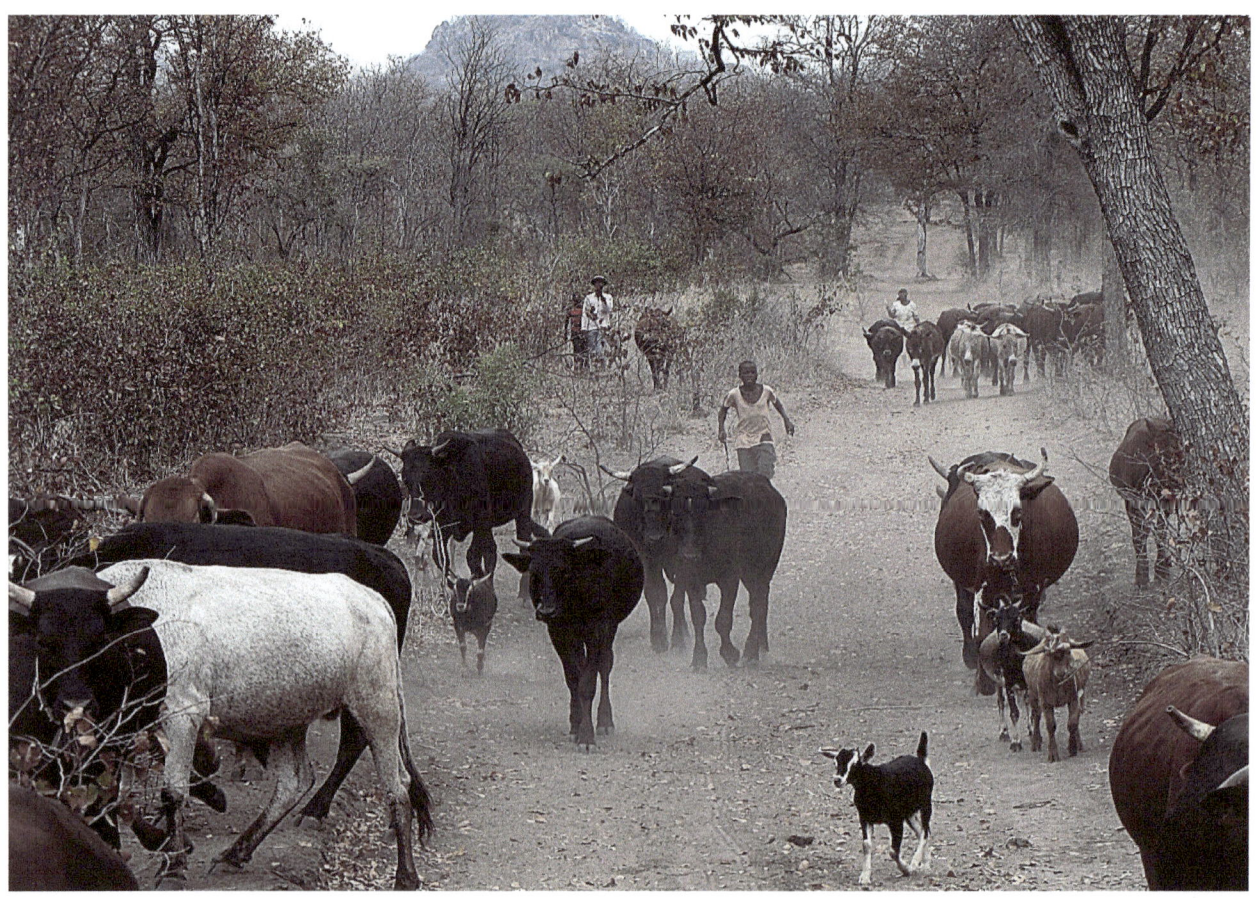

Young boys drive cattle to the river in southeastern Zimbabwe.

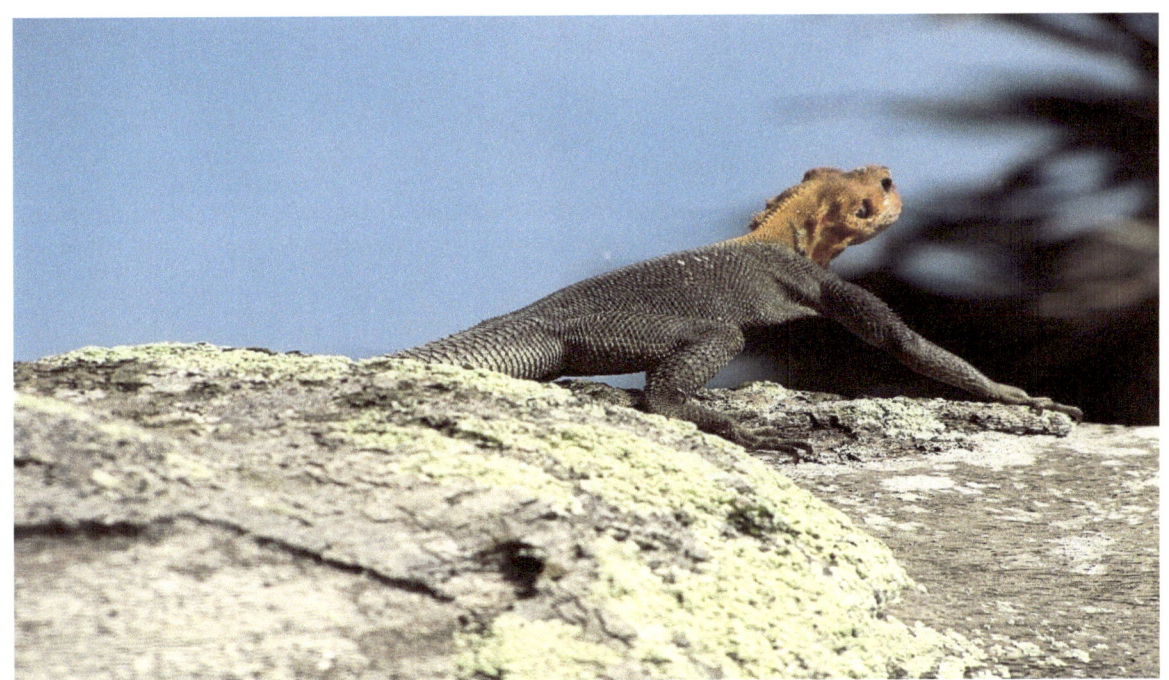

Colorful lizard on a rock in Cameroon.

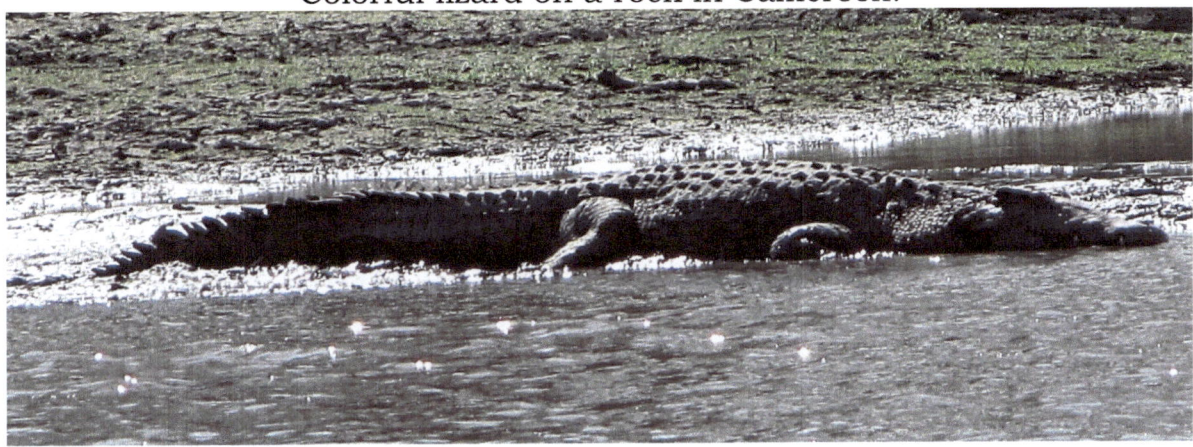

Crocodile lying in wait for prey in the shallows of the Zambezi River, Zimbabwe.

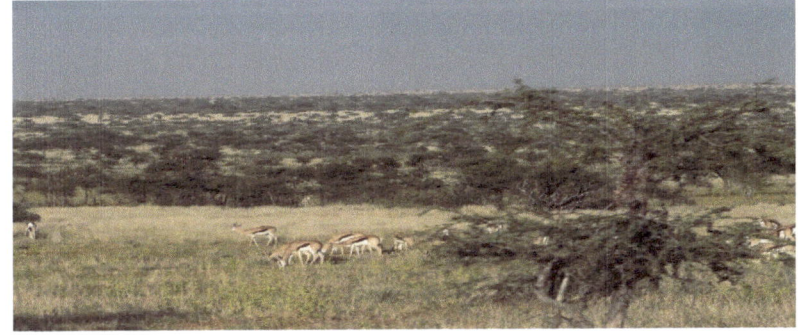

A herd of impala in the Kalahari Desert.

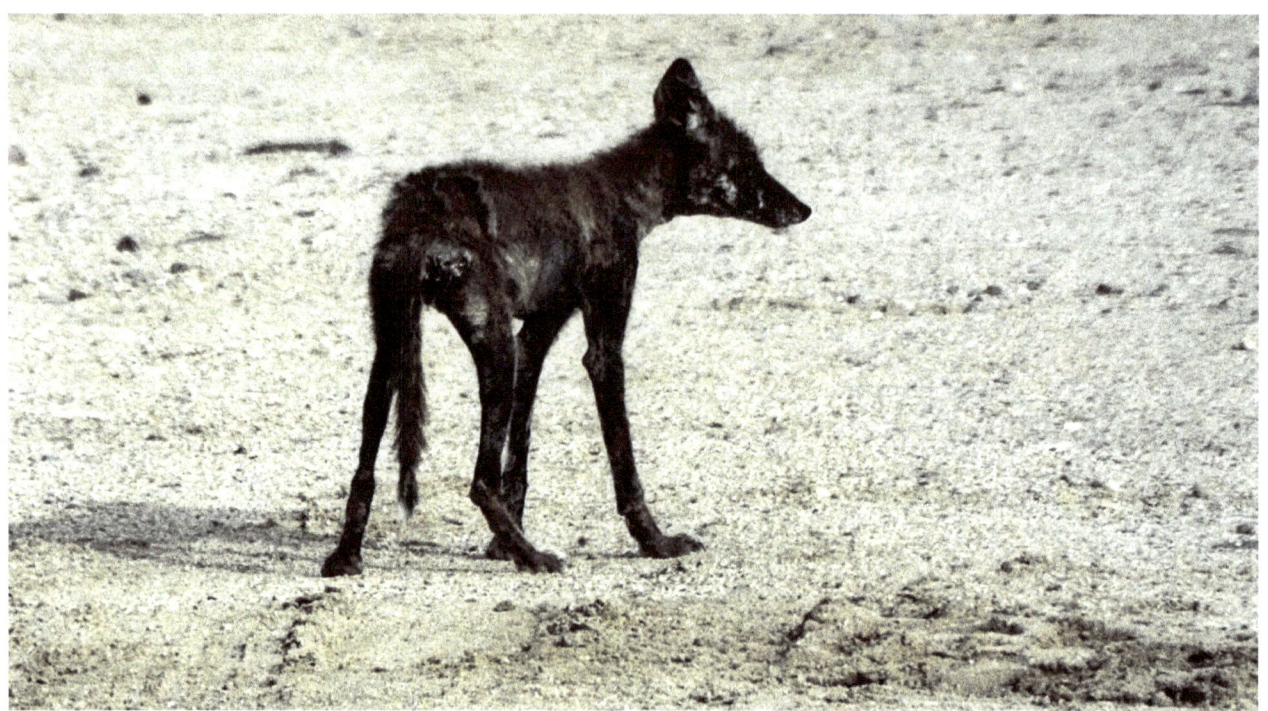

A denizen of the western desert, coyotes were seldom seen in inhabited areas until rampant development robbed them of much of their habitat. This one wandered into the main area of the army's Fort Irwin training center in the Mohave Desert.

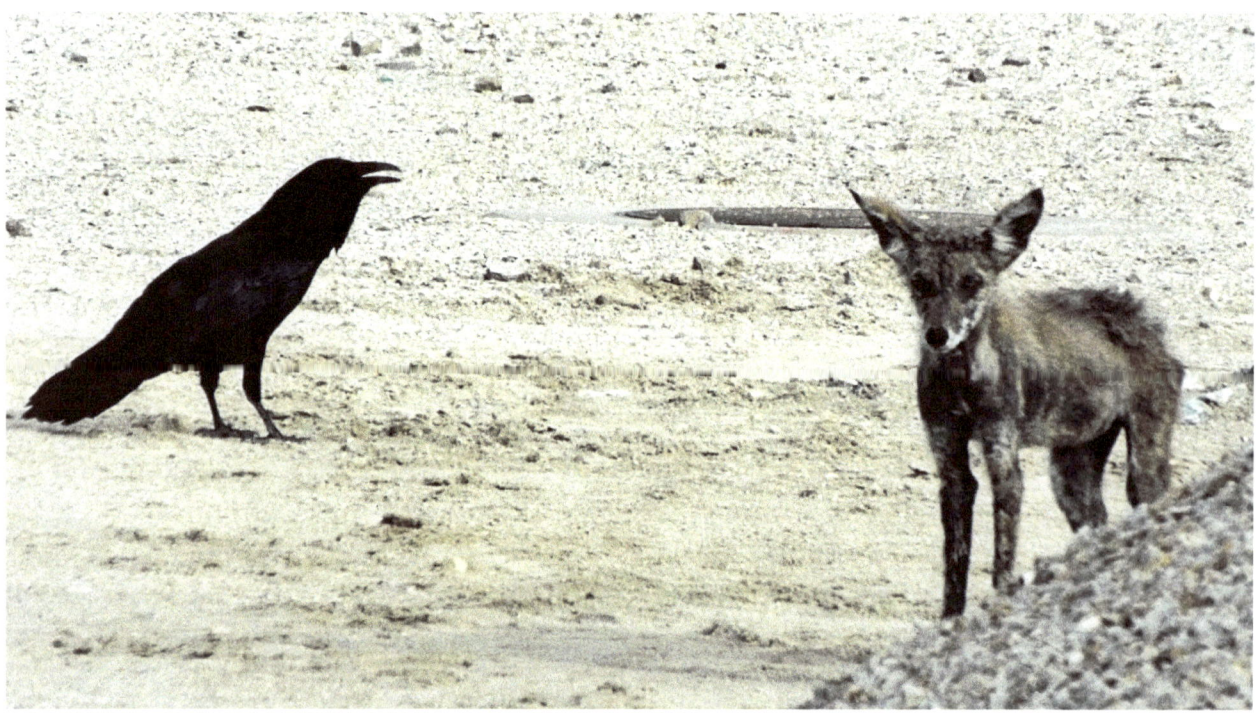

According to Native American legend, the coyote symbolizes trickery while the raven is a harbinger of death. Watching this raven in the Mojave Desert is eying this emaciated coyote and it's easy to see how the legend started.

Feathers, Fur and Flowers

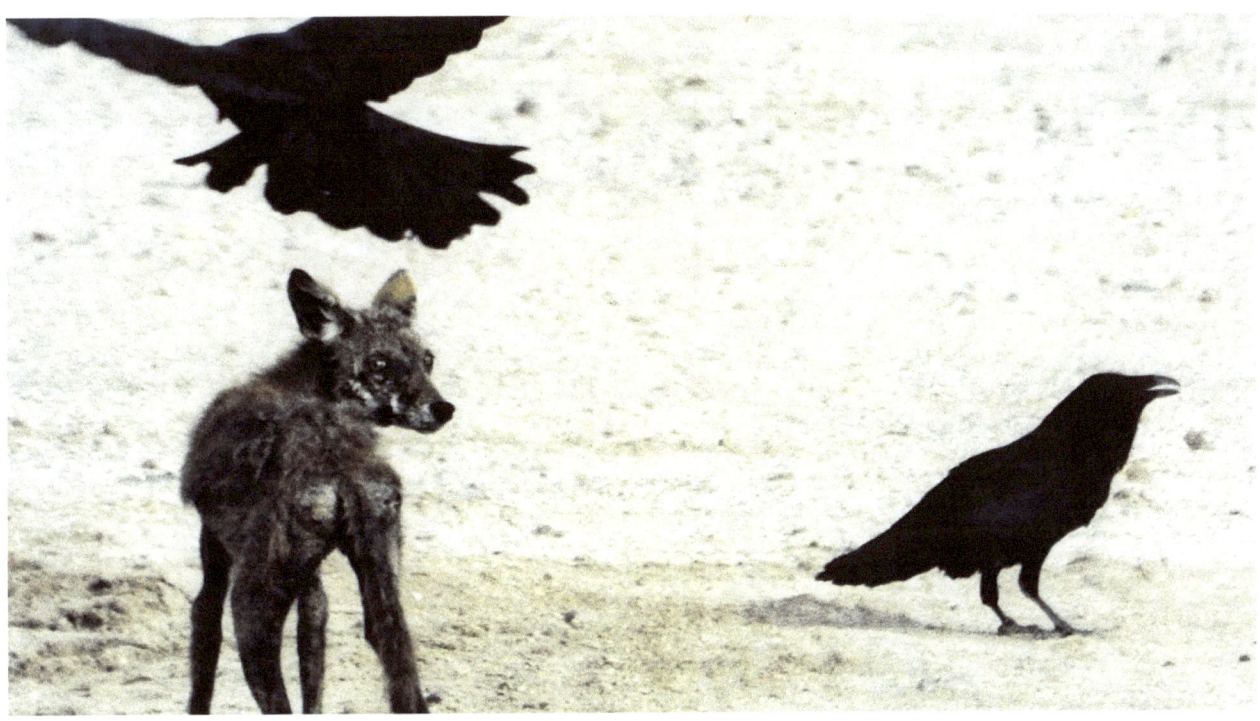

The ravens play with the coyote. His expression seems to indicate that he knows how things will end—not well for him.

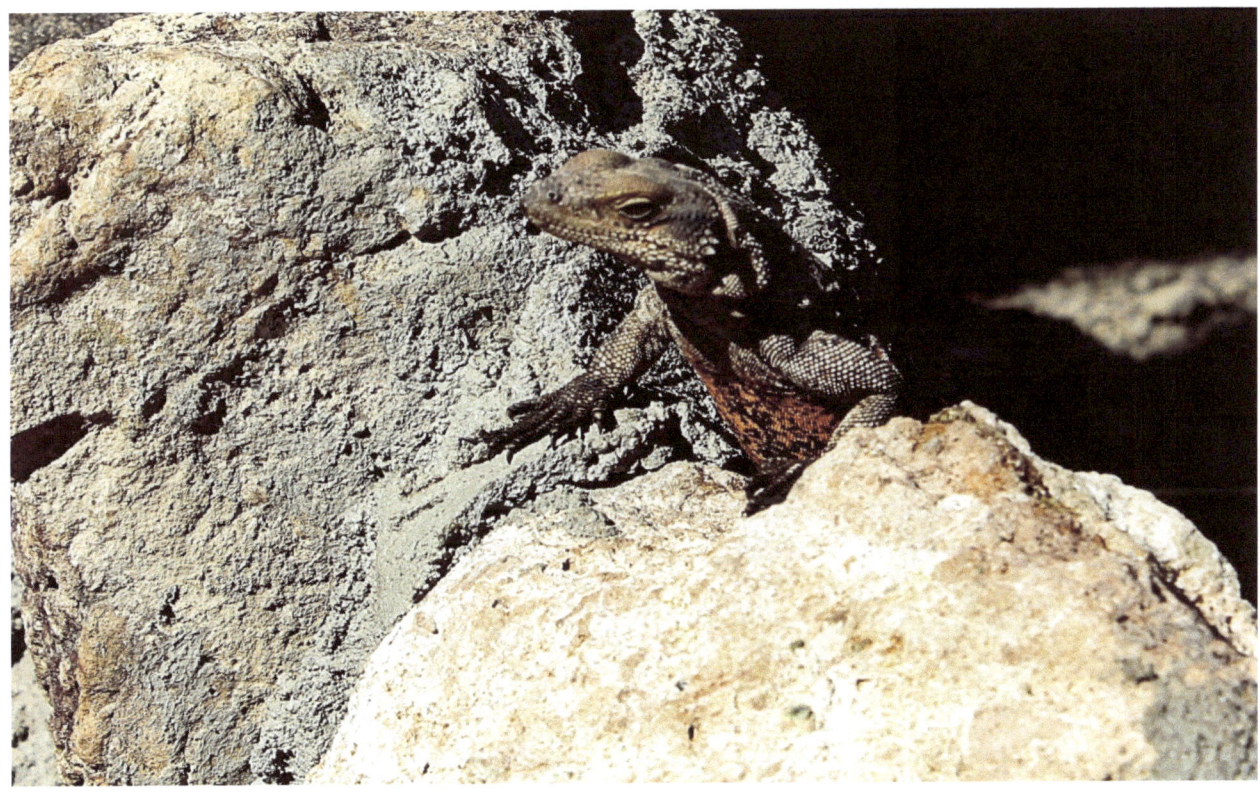

Another denizen of the western desert that stay-at-home folks seldom see, the Gila monster is normally shy. This one stayed out only for a few seconds, and when he spotted me taking pictures, darted back into the shadows.

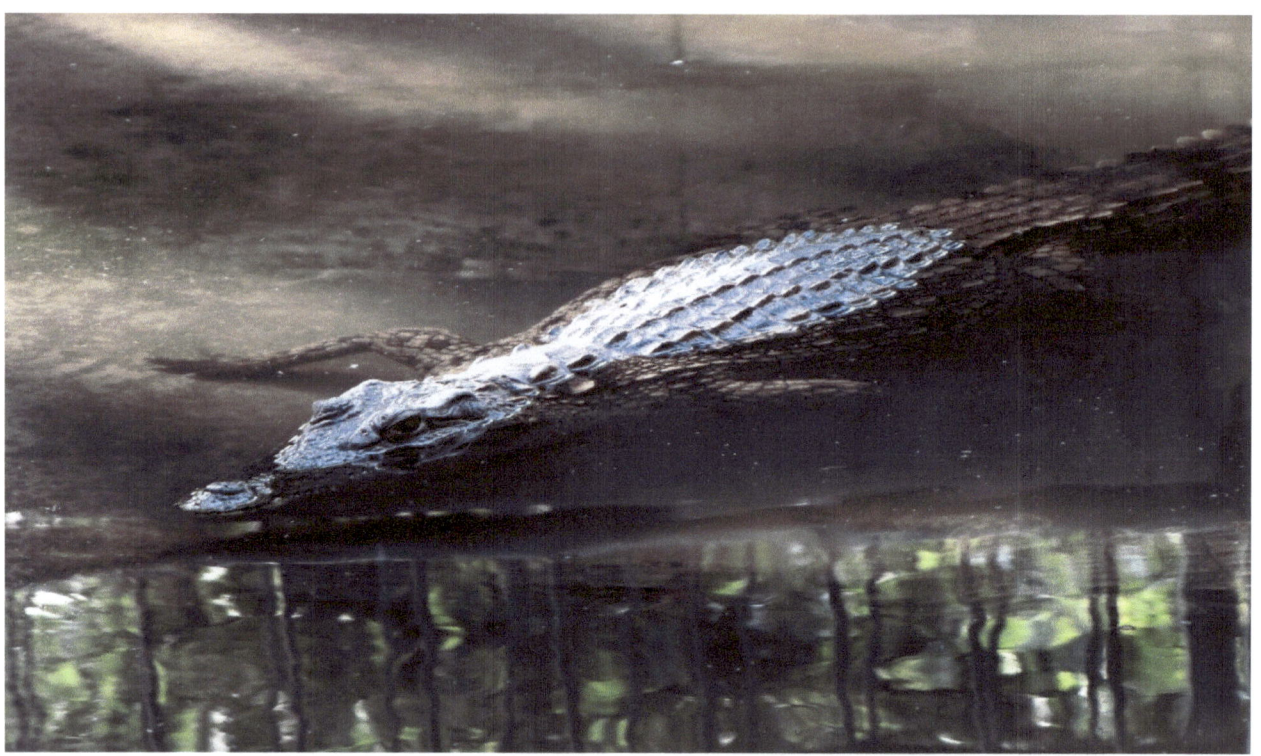

This is about as close as you might want to get to a crocodile. Fortunately, this big boy's attention was on something else.

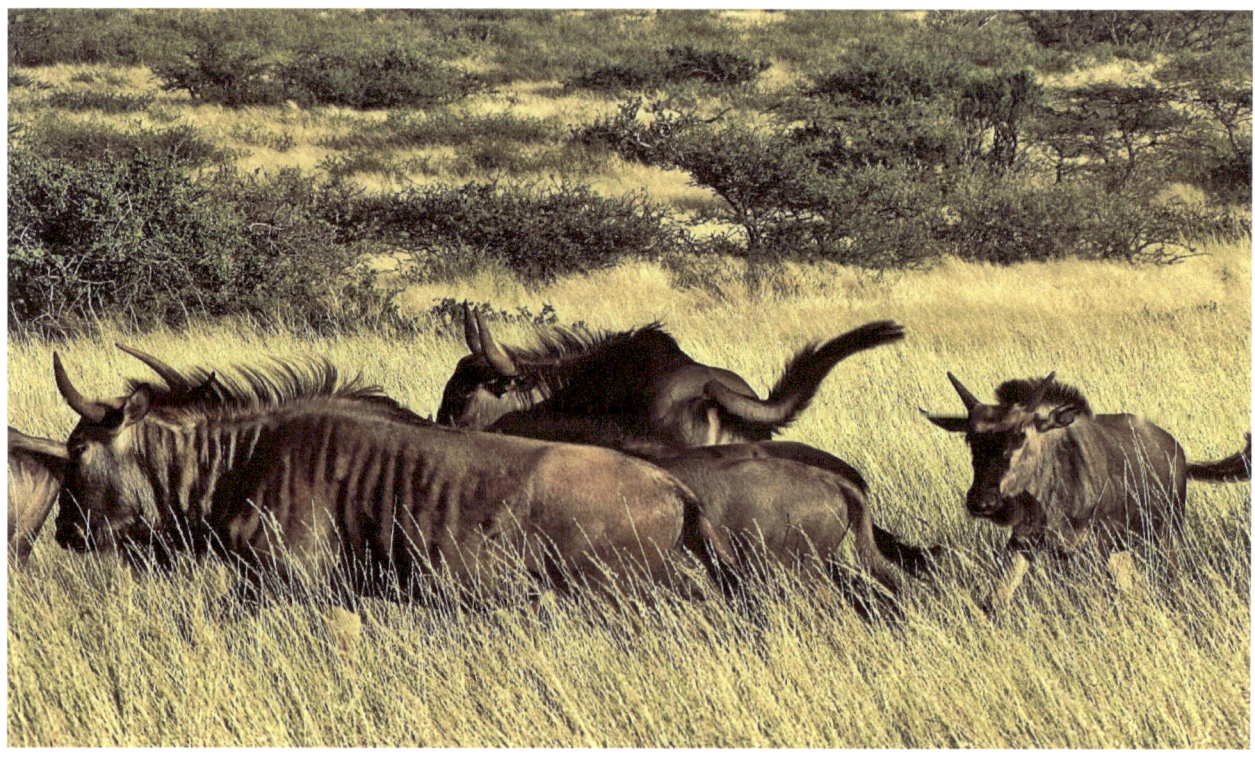

A herd of wildebeest romp across the Kalahari Desert.

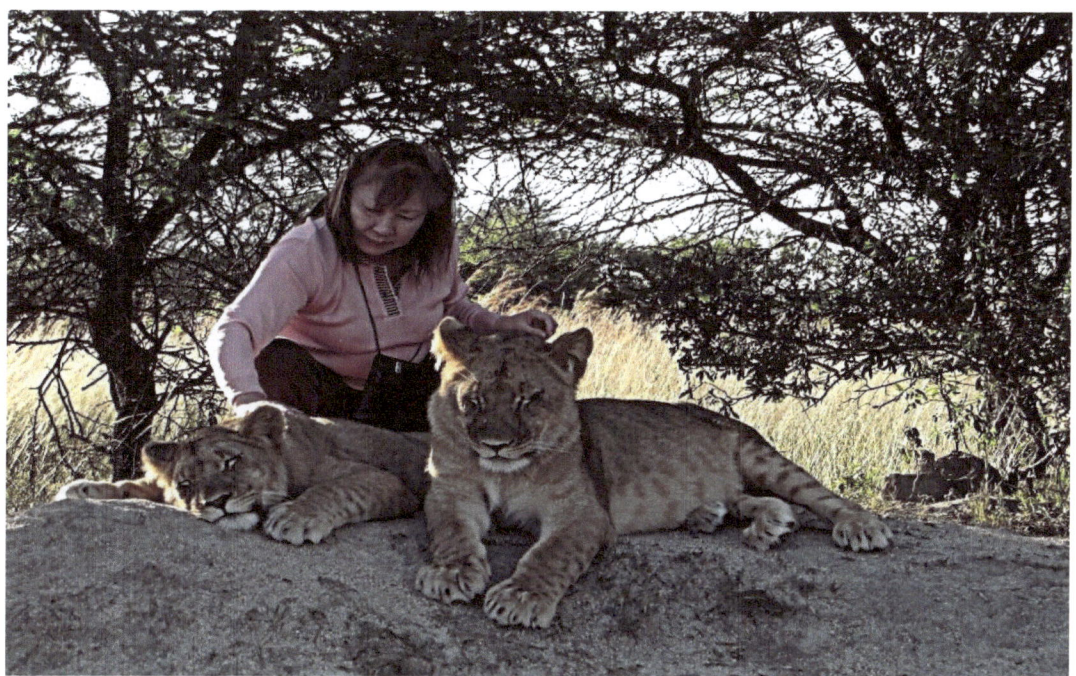

During our visit to Antelope Park in Zimbabwe, as we were walking with two lion cubs being prepared for reintroduction into the wild, the guide offered to let us pet them. I decided to just take pictures, but my wife, Myung, who had never seen a live lion before, couldn't resist.

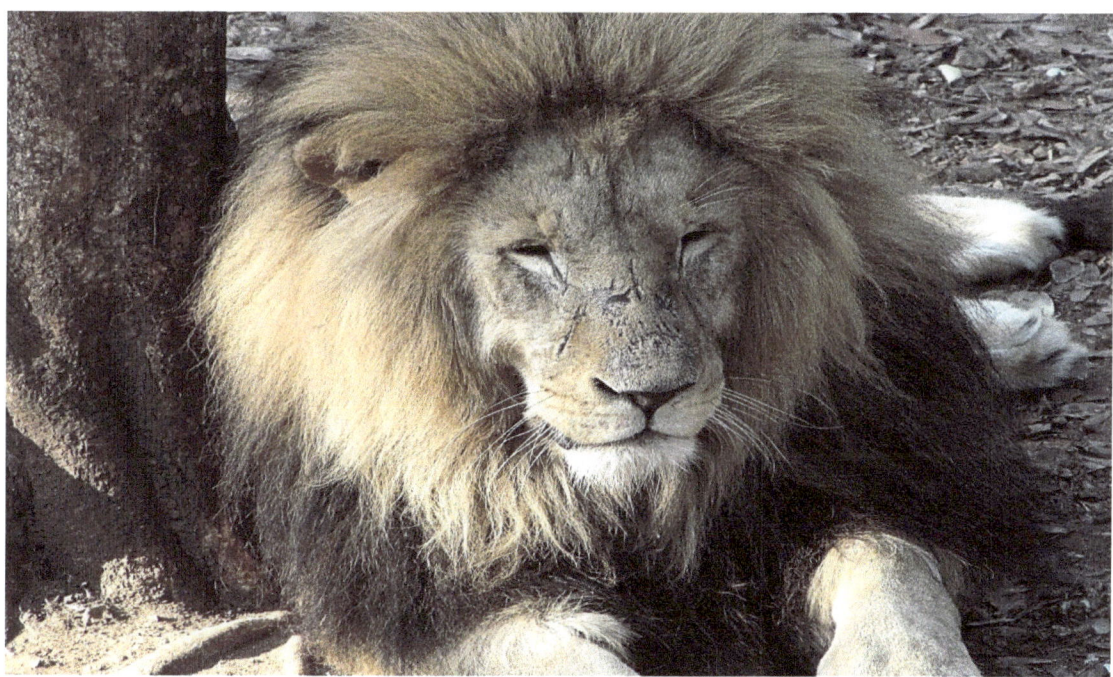

An old male lion in Hwange, Zimbabwe, doing what male lions are famous for, lying around doing nothing while the females hunt.

Charles Ray

FLOWERS

I'll start this section with an apology. While the title is 'Flowers,' I'm also including butterflies. There's a reason for that, which seemed a good reason at the time. I have a hard time thinking of butterflies as animals, even though technically I guess they *are* a part of the animal kingdom. They are so colorful, though, I felt they fit quite well in a section labeled flowers. So, enjoy.

In addition to playing loose on the definition of flower by including butterflies, some of the plants here—many in fact—are not actually flowers. But, you have to admit, like the first photo of a diaphanous bush in the Kalahari Desert, flower or not, they're beautiful. Well, I think so, at least. You will also notice that I like cacti. They're not everyone's cup of tea, but to me there's something majestic about this plant that can grow in such a harsh and unforgiving environment.

Oh, and while I am pretty good at recognizing, or researching and finding, the names of animals and birds, when it comes to plants, I'm pretty hopeless. I recognize roses and tulips, palm trees and oaks, but as for the rest, I don't have a clue where to even start identifying them, so I don't bother.

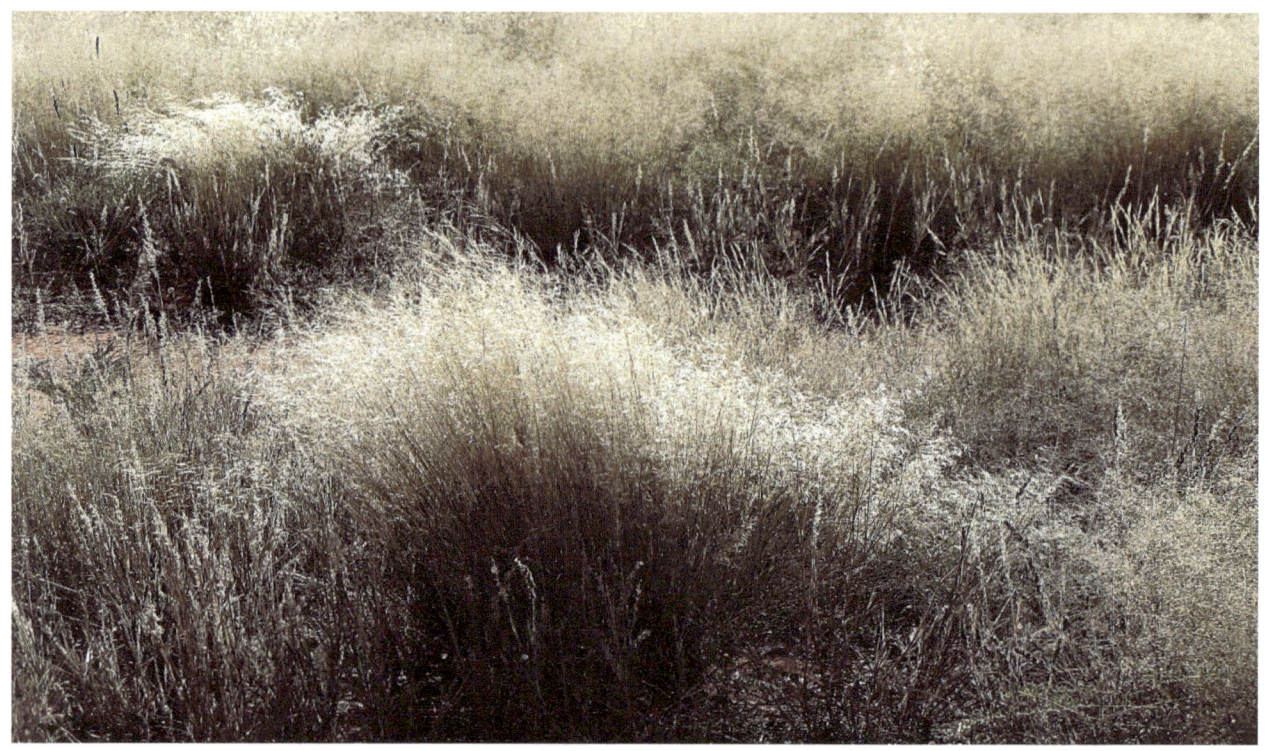

Feathery bush in the Kalahari seems to glow from within.

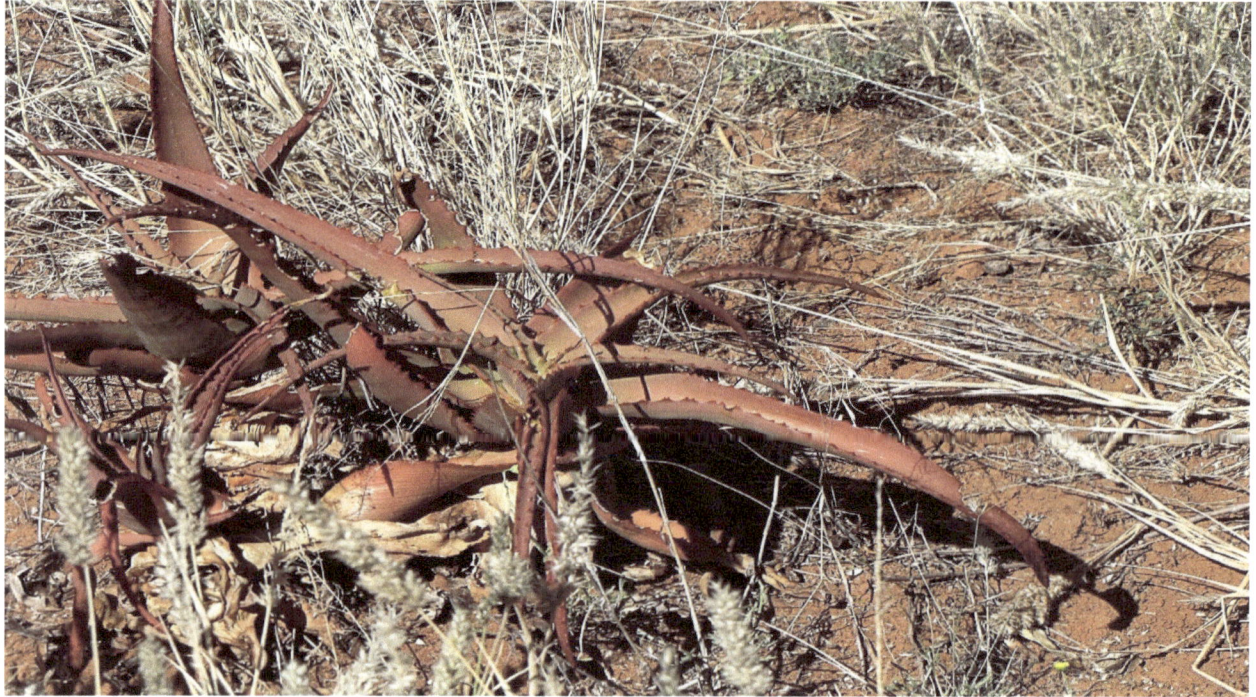

And then, there's this baby that looks positively menacing.

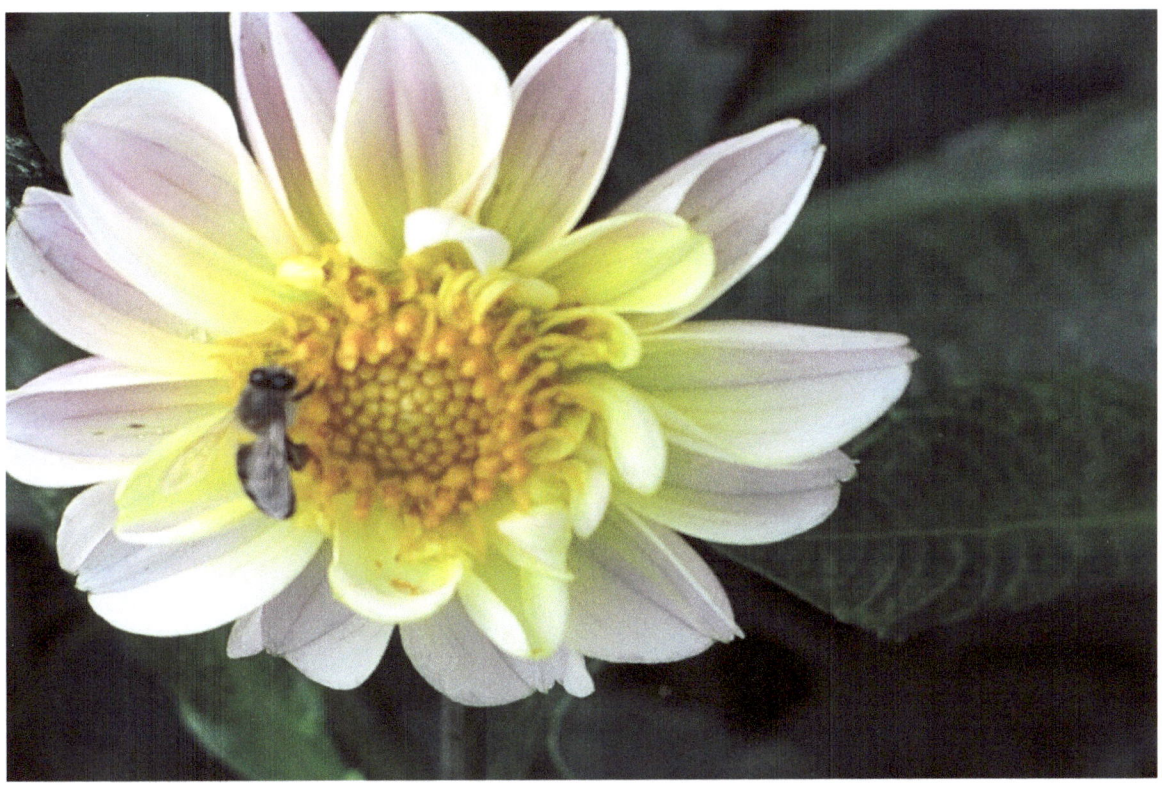

I actually don't recall where I took this photo, but I believe it was in Harare, Zimbabwe.

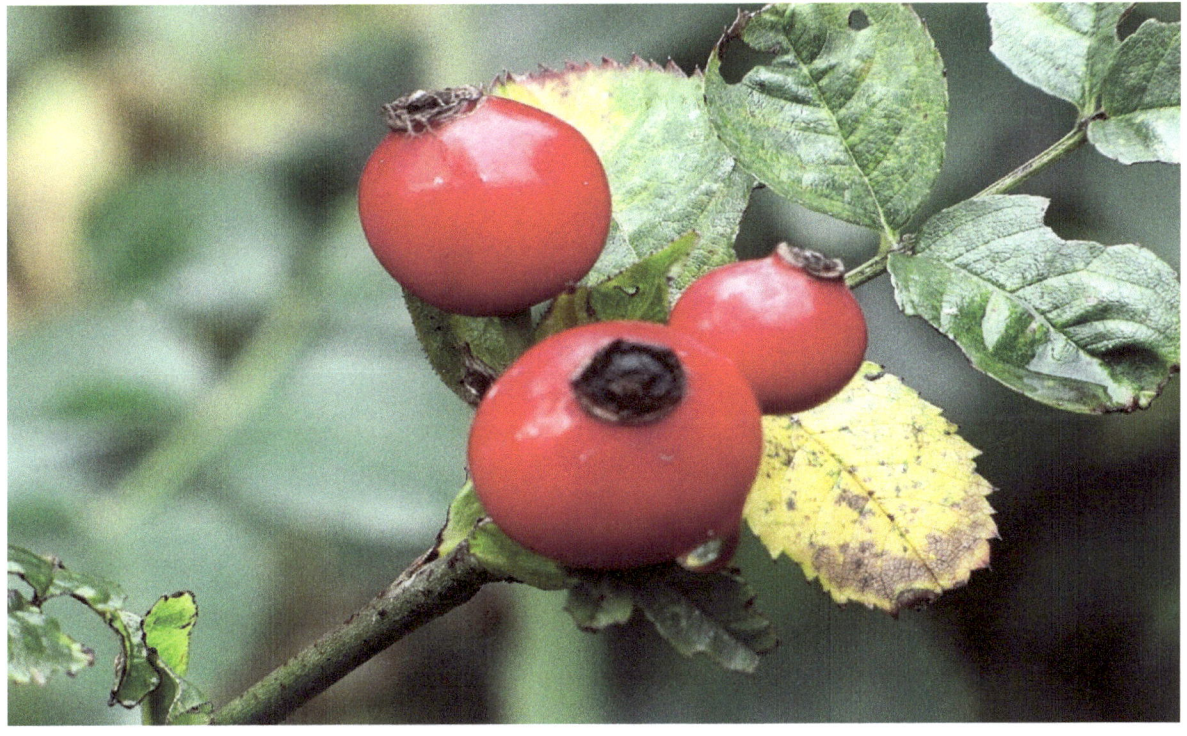

I stumbled upon these berries strolling through a forest in Kleve, Germany.

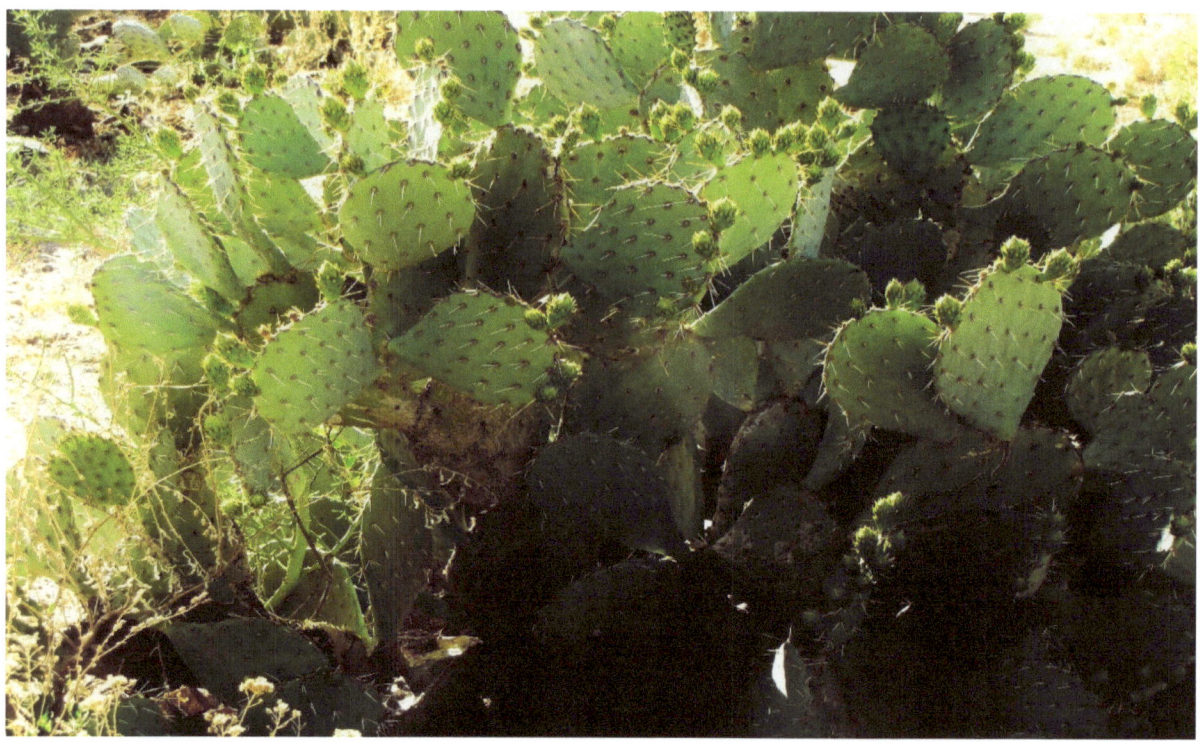

Cacti in the Sonora Desert in Arizona.

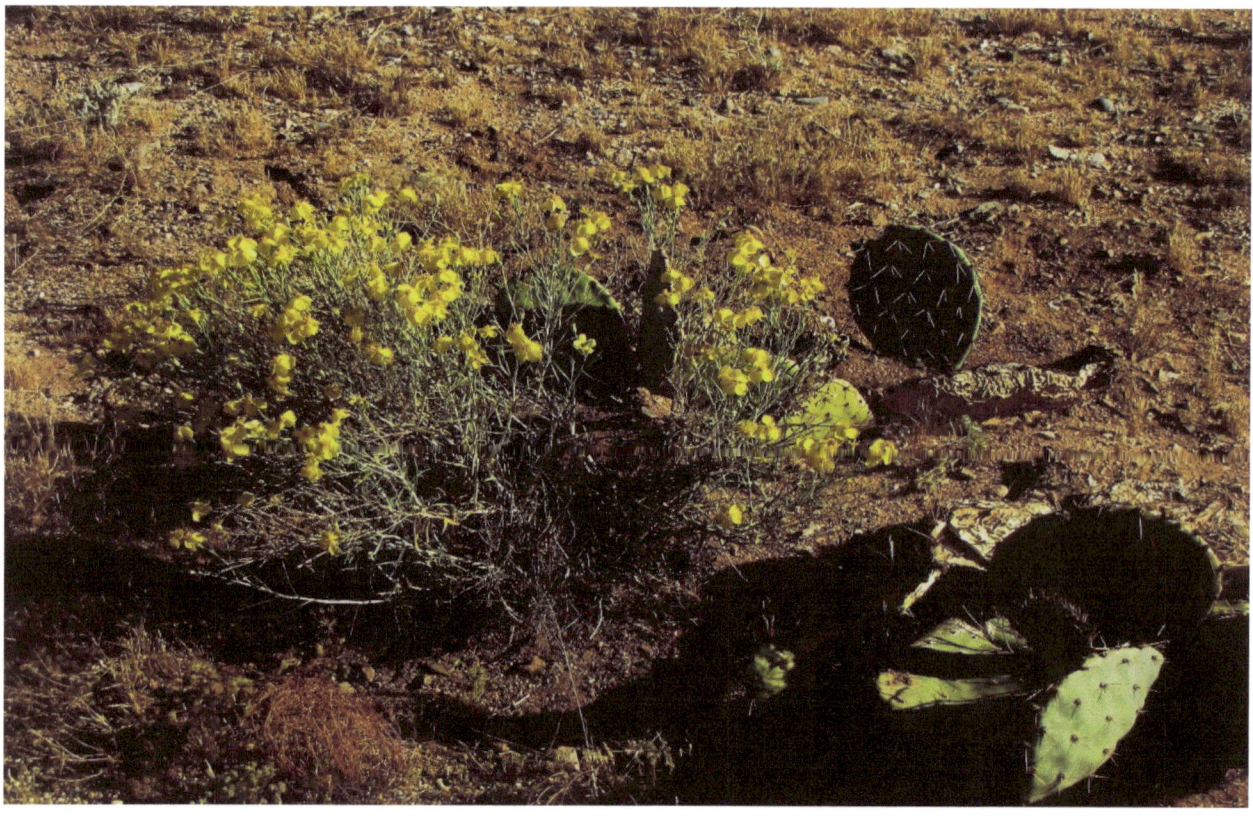

While you might not think of flowers in connection with deserts, this beautiful plant in the Sonora Desert shows that flowers bloom there too.

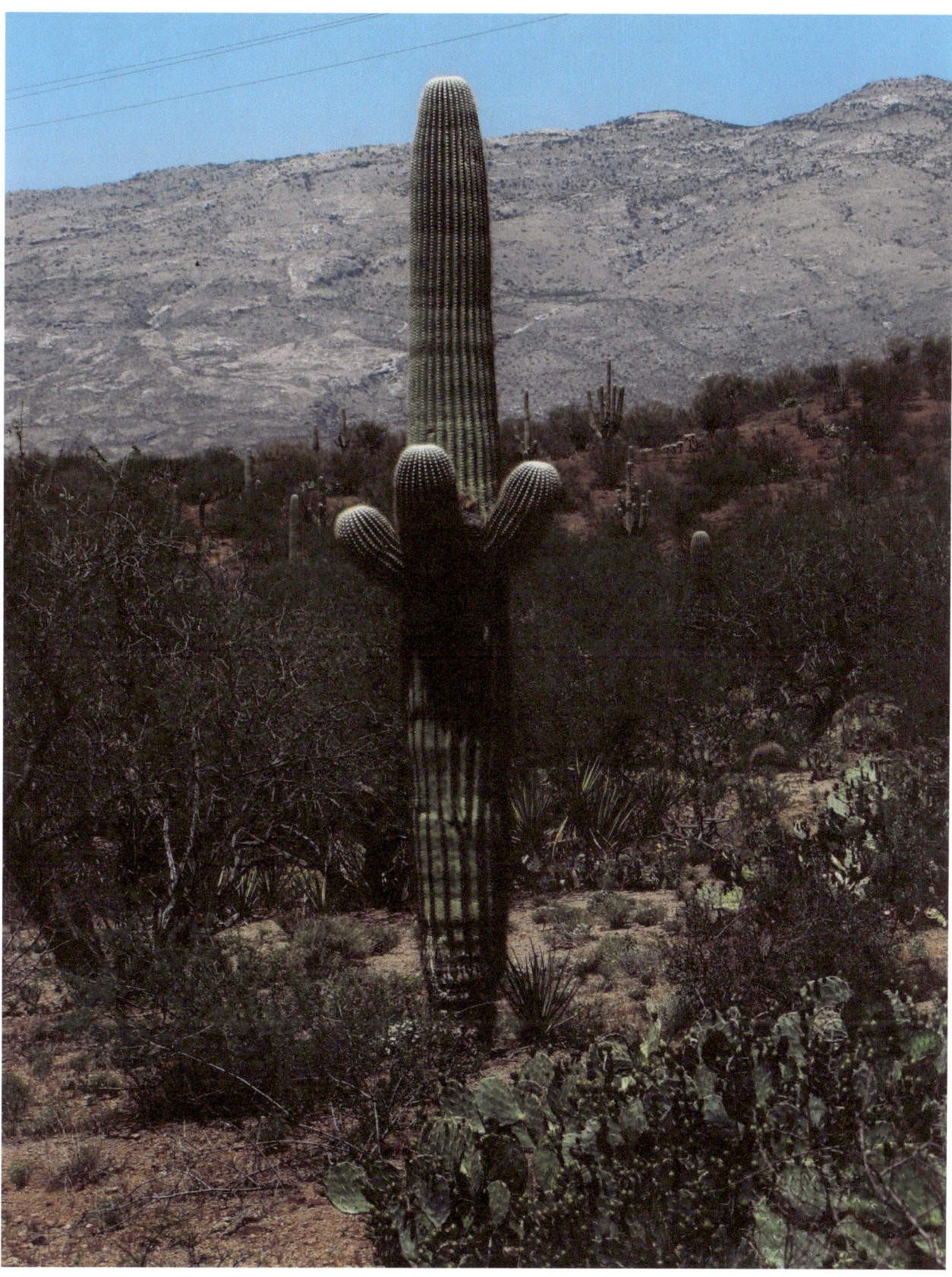

This saguaro cactus stands proud in eastern Arizona, near the New Mexico border.

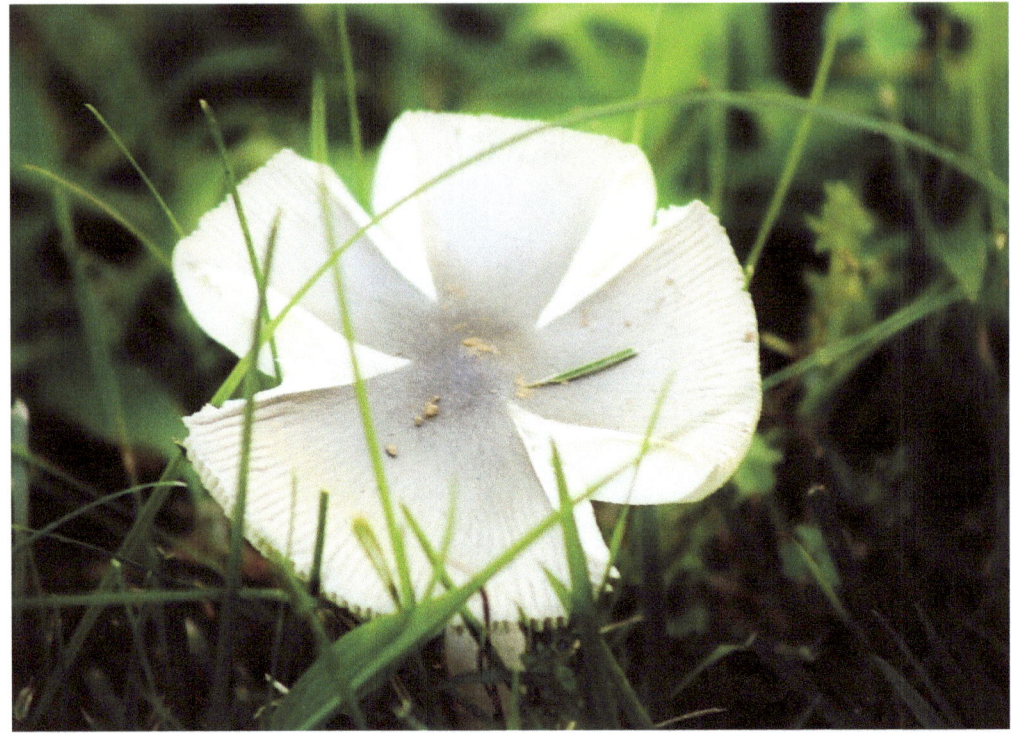

Not sure what this flower is called, but it grew in my yard in Harare, Zimbabwe.

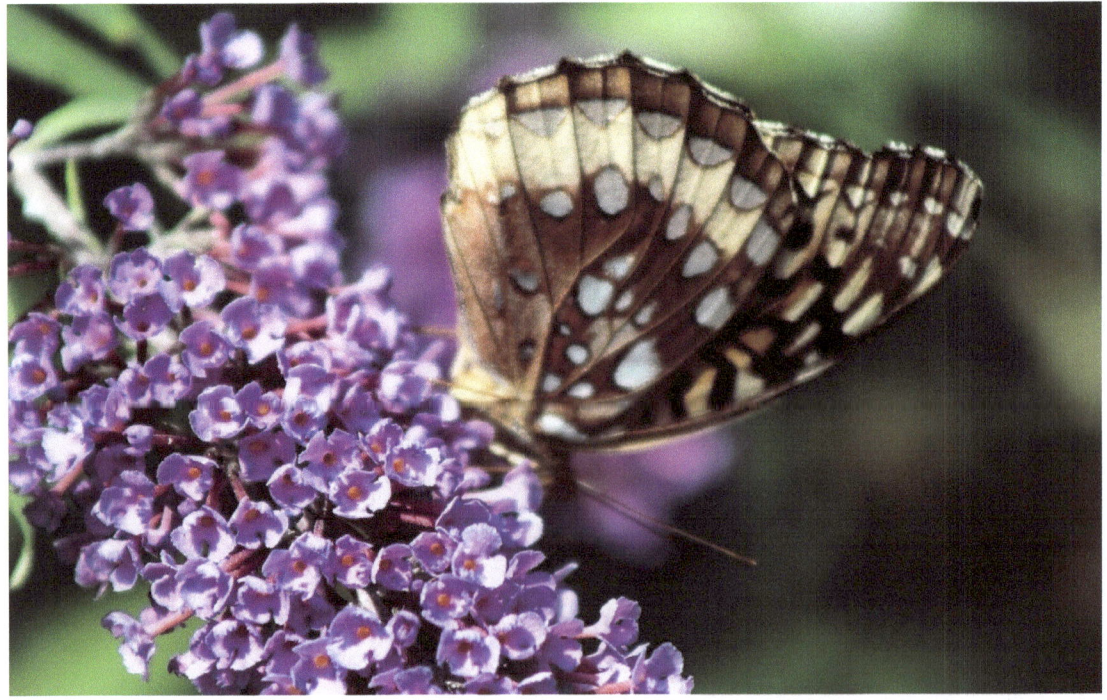

This lilac-colored flower grows in my neighbor's backyard in North Potomac, Maryland. It's a favorite haunt of several species of butterfly.

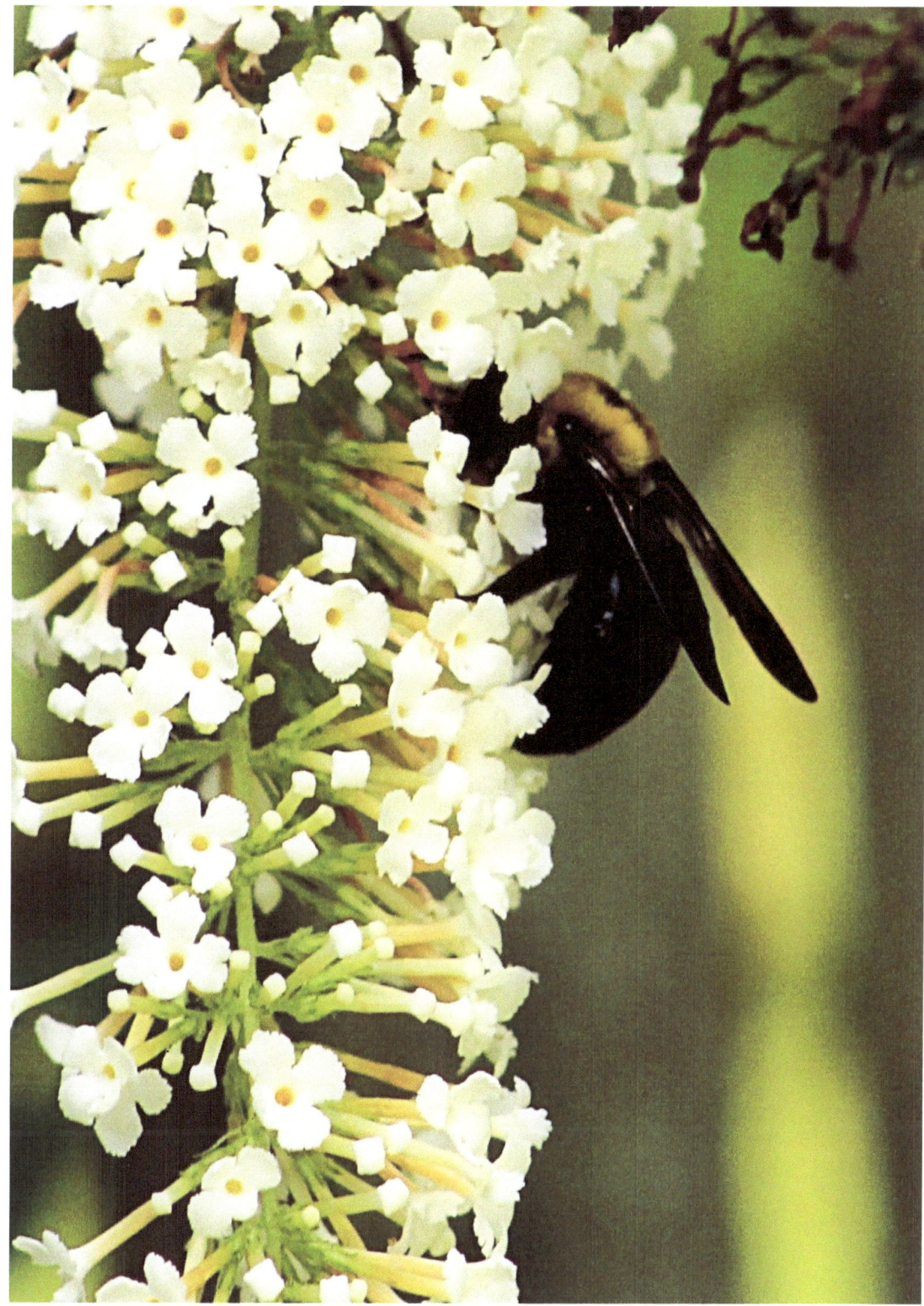

Another of my Maryland neighbor's flowers with a bee getting nectar.

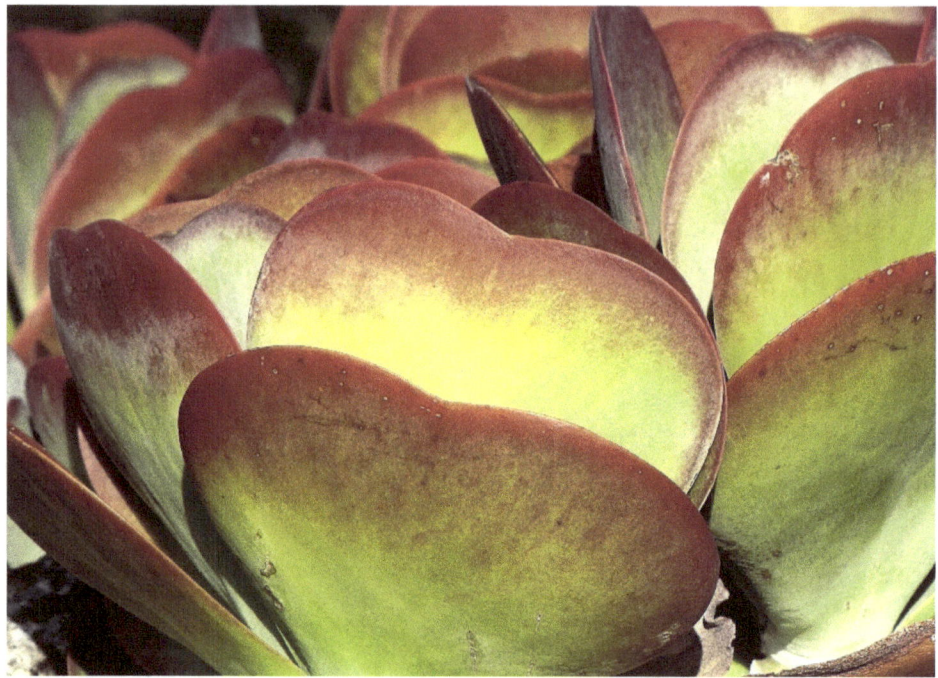

This plant grew outside my hotel in Pretoria. No idea what they're called, but they really caught my eye.

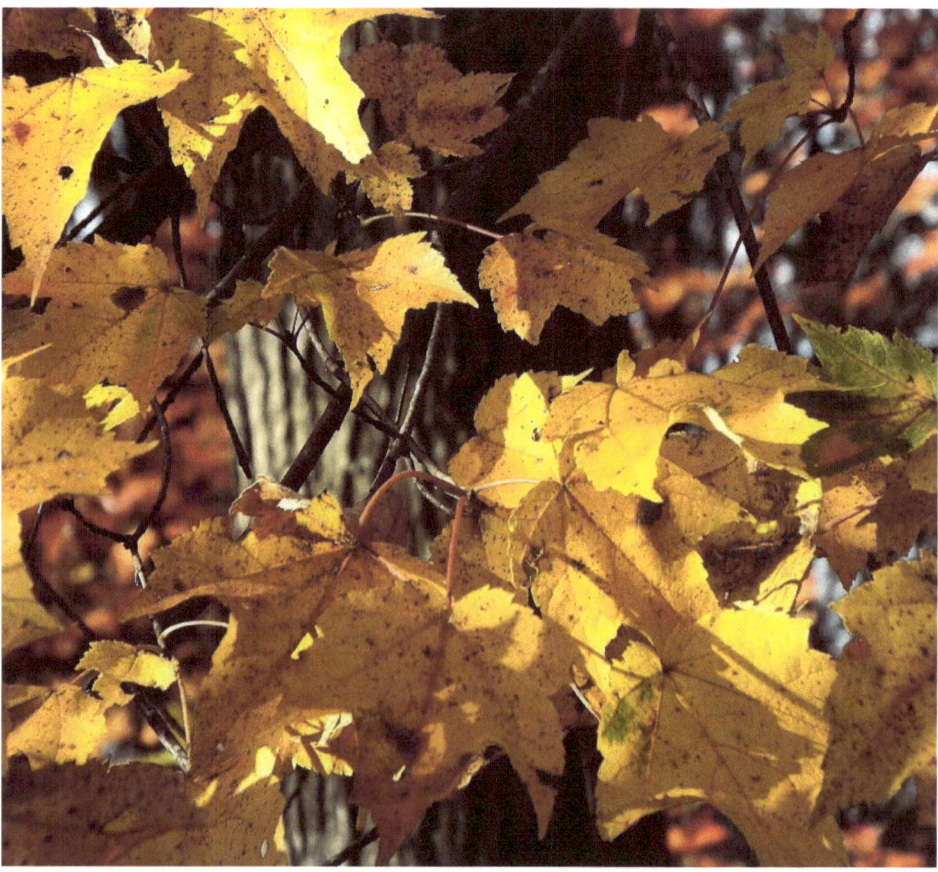

Okay, to they're leaves, not flowers, but you can't deny that autumn brings out the best colors in most trees.

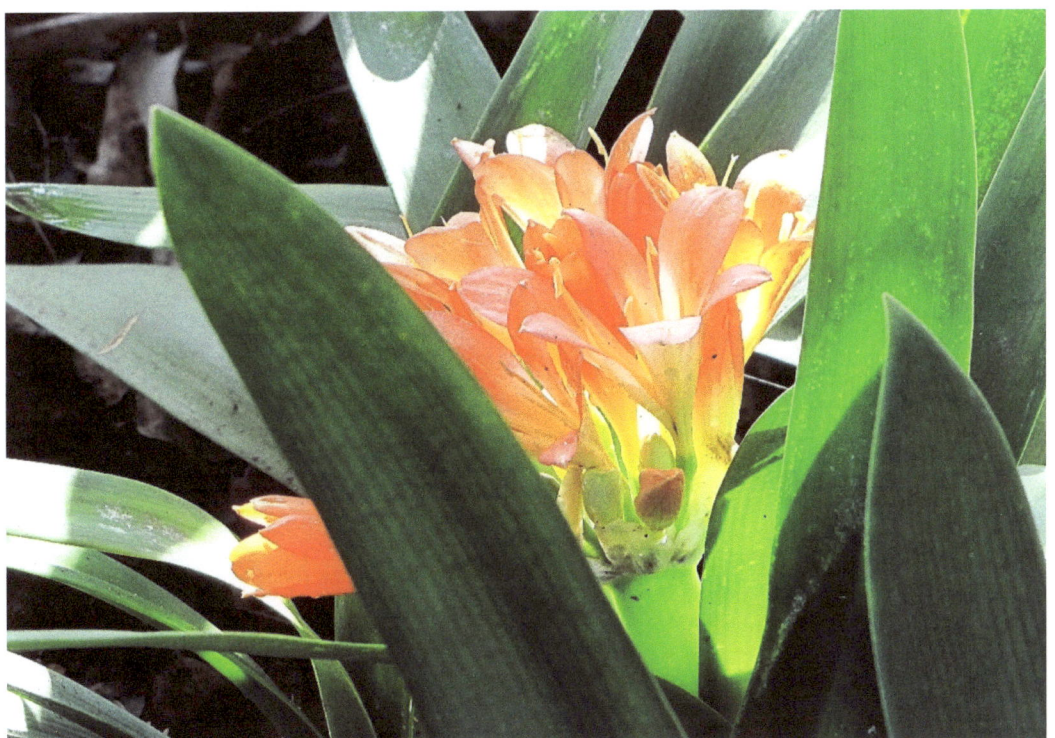

Another of the colorful flowers that grew in my yard in Harare.

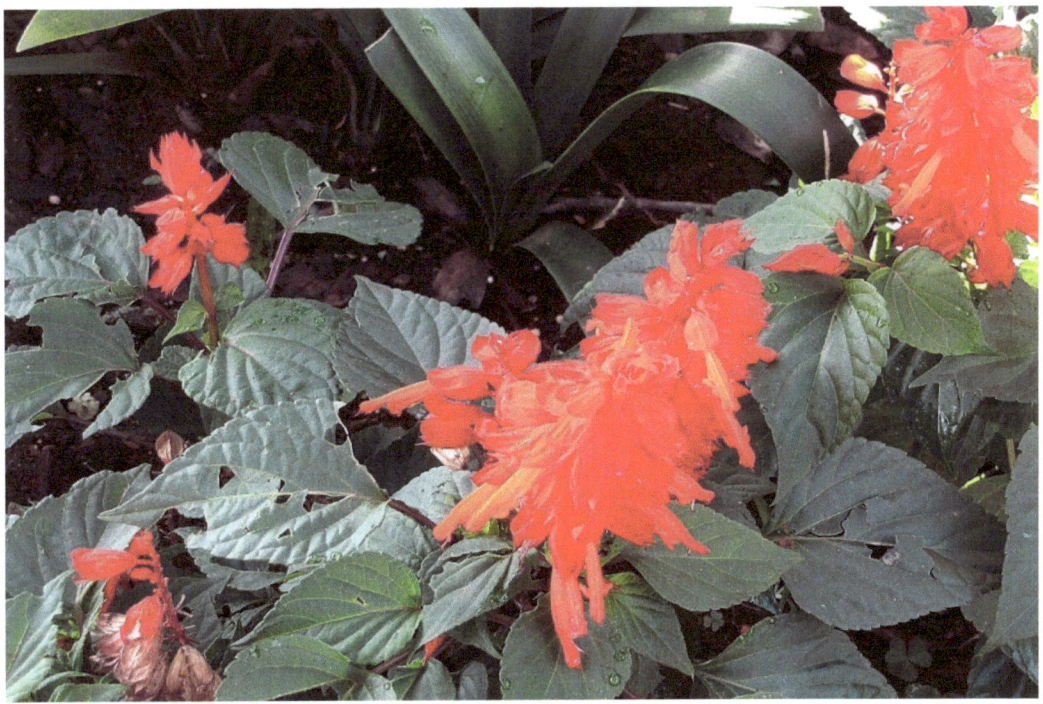

This orangish-red, or reddish orange is nice to look at on a cloudy day.

Charles Ray

NOTES ON EQUIPMENT, TECHNIQUES, AND OTHER ODDS AND ENDS

The following information is not intended to how-to, because, photography, like any other art form, is a highly subjective activity. I am sharing with you the equipment and techniques that I use, along with some other information that I think might be useful, just to give you an idea of how the pictures in this book came to be. If some of this is useful, I'm happy.

First, the equipment. I've owned cameras since my teens and have a large collection of old film cameras in the crawlspace above my garage. In 2002 I bought my first digital camera, a simple point-and-shoot device slightly larger than a deck of cards. In 2008, I bought my first digital SLR camera, and since then have gone to digital photography exclusively. My collection of digital cameras and equipment is beginning to rival my film camera collection.

This is what's usually in my camera bag:
- Canon PowerShot, SX10IS
- Canon EOS Rebel T5`
- FujiFilm Finepix S6800
- Canon EPS 18-55mm lens (for the T5)
- Canon 75-300mm lens (for the T5)
- Canon RS-60E3 remote shutter release
- Amazon Basics aluminum tripod
- Rangers Pro 58mm CPL filter
- Rangers Pro 58mm UV filter
- Rangers Pro filter adapter kit with gradated filters from dark to light
- Battery chargers (one for the T5 battery and another for rechargeable batteries for the other two cameras)
- Lens cleaning clothes
- Wet wipes (for when I accidentally get grease or dirt on camera or lens)
- Dessicant packs (won't keep things dry if it rains or you drop them in water, but great for humid climates to keep the inside of your gear bag relatively dry)
- Four gear bags (One for each camera, and one for the tripod)
- Note pad (for taking notes, of course)
- Pen and pencil (I prefer taking notes in pen, but when it's wet, or your pen runs out of ink, nothing beats a number two pencil)

I know this sounds like a lot of gear, but I seldom take more than two cameras with me on field trips. When I travel, I do take everything, but lock the gear I'm not using in the hotel room safe.

If you plan to get out into the wild, you need to consider how you should dress. Good sturdy hiking boots are a must, jeans or other sturdy pants, and a long-sleeve shirt. Even in summer, you might consider a windbreaker, because it can get chilly at night, and you wouldn't want to risk hypothermia. Oh, and for those of you who've never been in the desert, deserts get cold at night. You might be asking why long sleeves? On a sunny day, exposed arms can burn without you even being aware of it. Same goes for the back of the neck and the tips of the ears, so keep that collar snug, and wear a hat with a brim. I learned this lesson the hard way. When I lived in Vietnam, I played golf twice a week, and followed the local fashion of wearing a baseball cap. That worked great for protecting my forehead and nose, but at the end of three months of exposure I noticed that the tops of my ears were much darker than the rest. A checkup revealed that I had severe sunburn of the ear.

When you're in the field, be sure to have a good supply of water, especially in the summer or in the desert during the day. Dehydration can be deadly. Keep the sun screen and insect repellent handy wherever and whenever. You *can* get sunburn in winter, and even in cold weather, except sub-zero, there are biting and stinging pests around.

Another handy item of clothing is a hunter's vest, light weight for warm weather, and down-filled for winter. In addition to helping keep you warm, the extra pockets come in handy.

I do a certain amount of composing in the viewfinder, and use filters to help establish mood, but when you're photographing animals you sometimes have to shoot quick. That's where post-shot editing comes in. At the end of every day, I upload the day's pictures to my laptop, and use PhotoScape™, a simple, easy-to-use program that allows you to crop, manipulate color, and a lot of other things. You can download it free from www.photoscape.org/. PhotoScape also allows you to change the resolution of photos. Many publications require digital photos to be 300 dpi, while the average non-pro digital camera does 71 to 190 dpi. The term dpi means 'dots per inch,' and actually refers to the number of dots in a square inch a printer applies to paper. What is actually meant when someone says they want a 300 dpi photo is 'pixels per inch,' or ppi. Pixels are the dots that make up a digital photo. Why people still use dpi instead of ppi, and why it even matters, I don't know, but I routinely convert my photos to 300 dpi, because when I use photos with lower resolution in the books that I publish with CreateSpace™, I get annoying messages that these low-resolution photos might come out blurred in the final product. That's never happened, but I'd rather not tempt fate.

In addition to saving photos on my computer, I also back them up to a thumb drive, a stand-alone hard drive, and some to my DropBox™ cloud account.

The ones I think people will like, I also share on line. Sometimes to one of my blogs or web site:

My author page: www.charlesray-author.com

Charles Ray's Ramblings: http://charlieray45.wordpress.com/

Free flow of ideas is the cornerstone of democracy: http://charlesaray.blogspot.com/

Unsplash. A photo sharing site where a photographer's work is available for unrestricted download. https://unsplash.com/@charles_ray. I've been sharing many of my photos on this site for five years (currently have nearly 300 on the site), and they've been viewed 1.1 million times, at an average of 36,000 views per month. To date, over 20,000 of them have been downloaded by viewers.

I've had a Pro Account on Flickr since 2010, and have nearly 800 photos on that site: https://www.flickr.com/photos/charlesray45/. Photos from Flickr can also be downloaded and used, but unlike Unsplash, you have to get the photographer's permission first.

FineArtAmerica™ is a coop site that allows photographers and other artists to showcase their work for sale, either as standalones, or part of a product design. Check out my portfolio at https://fineartamerica.com/profiles/2-charles-ray.html.

I have my own on-line stores featuring products designed around my art. Uhuru by Charles Ray is at https://www.zazzle.com/uhurubycharlesray, and Designs by Ray, which is also a Zazzle store, is at https://www.zazzle.com/designs_by_ray.

I hope you see where I'm going with this. Photography can be a fun hobby, but if you develop your skill and have the energy and desire to promote your work, you can also make a little money from it. Who knows, you just might be the next Ansel Adams, and become world famous.

There you have it. A leg of my photographic journey starting from the time I pressed the shutter release on my mother's Kodak Brownie. I hope you've enjoyed the photos here, and if you did, that you'll take a moment to post a few words of review on Amazon, Goodreads, or any other retail book site.

Bon journee.

Charles Ray

Books by this author:

Al Pennyback mysteries
Color Me Dead
Memorial to the Dead
Deadline
Dead, White, and Blue
A Good Day to Die
The Day the Music Died
Die, Sinner
Deadly Intentions
Death by Design
Till Death Do Us Part
Deadly Dose
Dead Man's Cove
Dead Men Don't Answer
Deadly Paradise
Kiss of Death
Death in White Satin
Death and Taxis
Deadbeat
A Deadly Wind Blows
Death Wish
Deadly Vendetta
A Time to Kill, A Time to Die
Dead Ringer
Death of Innocence
Dead Reckoning
Murder on the Menu
Over My Dead Body
Bad Girls Don't Die
A Deal to Die For

Ed Lazenby mysteries
Butterfly Effect
Coriolis Effect
The Cat in the Hatbox
Negative Side Effects
Murder is as Easy as ABC

Buffalo Soldier series
Buffalo Soldier: Trial by Fire
Buffalo Soldier: Homecoming

Buffalo Soldier: Incident at Cactus Junction
Buffalo Soldier: Peacekeepers
Buffalo Soldier: Renegade
Buffalo Soldier: Escort Duty
Buffalo Soldier: Battle at Dead Man's Gulch
Buffalo Soldier: Yosemite
Buffalo Soldier: Comanchero
Buffalo Soldier: Range War
Buffalo Soldier: Mob Justice
Buffalo Soldier: Chasing Ghosts
Buffalo Soldier: The Piano
Buffalo Soldier: Family Feud
Buffalo Soldier: The Lost Expedition

Other fiction
Angel on His Shoulder
She's No Angel
Child of the Flame
Pip's Revenge
Wallace in Underland
Further Adventures of Wallace in Underland
Dead Letter and Other Tales
The White Dragons
The Dragon's Lair
Dragon Slayer
The Last Gunfighters
The Culling
Frontier Justice: Bass Reeves, Deputy U.S. Marshal
Angel on His Shoulder-Revised Edition
Battle at the Galactic Junkyard
Mountain Man
Devil's Lake
Vixen
Wagons West: Daniel's Journey
Wagons West: Trinity
Awakening
Fatal Encounters: The Adventures of Bass Reeves, Deputy U.S. Marshal
Chase the Sun

Nonfiction
Things I Learned from My Grandmother About Leadership and Life
Taking Charge: Effective Leadership for the Twenty-first Century
Grab the Brass ring
African Places: A Photographic Journey

Through Zimbabwe and southern Africa
A Portrait of Africa
There's Always a Plan B
In the Line of Fire: American Diplomats in the Trenches
Advice for the Insecure Writer
Looking at Life Through My Lens
Ethical Dilemmas and the Practice of Diplomacy
Making America Grate Again
DC Street Art
Dead Letters and Other Tales: Revised edition
Feathers, Fur, and Flowers

Children's books
The Yak and the Yeti
Samantha and the Bully
Molly Learns to Share
Where is Teddy?
Catie and Mister Hop-Hop
Tommy Learns to Count
Catie Goes to School

About the Author

Charles Ray has been writing fiction since his teens. He won a Sunday school magazine writing contest when he was thirteen and having his byline on a short story published in a national publication forever hooked him on writing. During his time in the army (1962-1982) he often moonlighted as a newspaper or magazine journalist and was the editorial cartoonist for the Spring Lake (NC) News, a weekly newspaper, during the 1970s. In addition to his writing, he was an artist/cartoonist and photographer for a number of publications, including Ebony, Eagle and Swan, and Essence, and had a monthly cartoon feature and did several covers for Buffalo, a now-defunct magazine that was dedicated to showcasing the contributions of African-Americans to the country's military history.

After retiring from the army, he joined the U.S. Foreign Service, and served as a diplomat in posts in Asia and Africa until his retirement in 2012. He has worked and traveled throughout the world (Antarctica is the only continent he hasn't visited), and now, as a full-time writer, continues to globetrot looking for interesting things to write about, draw, or take pictures of.

A native of Texas, he now calls Maryland home. For more on his writing and other projects, check one of the following Web sites:

http://charlesaray.blogspot.com
http://charlieray45.wordpress.com
http://www.twitter.com/charlieray45
http://www.facebook.com/charlieray45
http://www.flickr.com/photos/charlesray45/
http://www.viewbug.com/member/charlesray

You can also order some of my books through my author's website: http://charlesray-author.com/

Authors write to be read, and that can only happen when readers are made aware of the books available. Reviews are one way this happens. If you liked this book, please leave a review, even if only a few words, on Amazon or Goodreads.

www.ingramcontent.com/pod-product-compliance
Lightning Source LLC
Chambersburg PA
CBHW051205220526
45473CB00003B/907